Unlock The Corporate Mindset

Monika Black & Tomer Yogev

Copyright © 2017 by Monika Black & Tomer Yogev.

All rights reserved.

No part of this book may be reproduced, stored in a retrieval system, or transmitted in any form or by any means, electronic, mechanical, photocopying, recording, scanning, or otherwise, except as permitted under Section 107 or 108 of the 1976 United States Copyright Act, without the prior written permission of the authors.

The authors have made every effort to provide accurate Internet addresses at the time of publication. Neither the publisher nor author assumes any responsibility for errors or for changes that occur after publication. Further, the publisher and author do not have any control and do not assume any responsibility for third-party websites or their content.

Limit of Liability/Disclaimer of Warranty: While the authors have used their best efforts in preparing this book, they make no representations or warranties with respect to the accuracy or completeness of the contents of this book and specifically disclaim any implied warranties of merchantability or fitness for a particular purpose. No warranty may be created or extended by sales representatives or written sales materials. The advice and strategies contained herein may not be suitable for your situation. You should consult with a professional where appropriate. Neither the publisher nor the author shall be liable for damages arising herefrom.

First edition: November 2017

ISBN: 1979522618
ISBN-13: 978-1979522618

To our dear friends and chosen family.
You know who you are.
We cherish you.

> DEFINE SUCCESS ON YOUR OWN TERMS, ACHIEVE IT BY YOUR OWN RULES, AND BUILD A LIFE YOU'RE PROUD TO LIVE.
>
> — ANNE SWEENEY

Contents

i	**Preface**
iii	Monika's Preface
vi	Tomer's Preface
viii	TandemSpring's Preface
1	**Let's Get Started**
11	**The Corporate Mindset**
15	What Is The Corporate Mindset?
22	Knowing The Corporate Mindset When You See It
26	Take Your "Shit" And Take Your "Hill" And Just Leave Us Alone!
31	**Unleashing From The Corporate Mindset And The Linear Illusion Of Success**
37	Bringing Your Whole Self To Work
40	Becoming A Productive Leader
43	Defying The Linear Model of Success
46	Rejecting The Non-Rules Of The Corporate Mindset
48	Shifting To Your Own Model of Success
50	Measuring Your Truth, By Your Truth
51	**The Evolution To Radical Leadership**
56	Superpowers Activate!
63	Get The Freak Out Of Here
69	Risking It All, But For All The Right Reasons
74	Who First? Me First?!
78	The Trust Factor
87	Where Is Your Finish Line?
93	The Fear Of The Illusion That Is Success
100	Turn Fear Of Conflict Into Windows Of Opportunity
111	Being Accountable To You
118	Your Authentic Presence As A Leader
124	Success On The Brighter Side Of Leadership
131	Conclusion

PREFACE

Monika's Preface

I arrived at college full of excitement and eager to spread my wings and become the fullest version of myself. But, even before I had gotten my dorm room arranged the way I wanted, I was already noticing a disturbing trend: people appeared to feel that they simply did not have choice. So many were succumbing to peer pressure and I could feel their conflict about it. I couldn't understand it. From this feeling of lack of choice, I'd watch my fellow students make all sorts of unproductive decisions, from tagging along to parties they should never have gone to, to dating people for status and not for any level of real interest.

Now, I'm not so prudish as to think every decision in college must be "productive" in the traditional sense. But they also do not have to be born out of insecurity or the sense that we cannot do what we really want to do. I was saddened by the number of people who felt compelled to conform. Some did it in the name of being cool, others to hold onto a friend, while others appeared directionless altogether. I kept asking myself wasn't the whole point of college to help young adults learn who they really are and how they want to lead in the world?

Anyone who knows me from my college days can attest that I led with a fierce sense of justice for myself and others. We could debate just how well developed my leadership skills were at that point in my life, and I may not care to know what my peers called it at the time. But just about everything I did and said was done with the intention of helping people see that they always had choice.

Naively, as I left college and entered the working world, I thought that the pressure to be someone else in life would dissipate with age, time, money and experience. Surely, adults were free to make the decisions that they wanted to make, right?! As I entered corporate life, I was again shocked to find people of all ages, titles, and levels of "success" continuing to wrestle with the same types of issues I saw in college: Who am I, really? Who do I have to be to become successful? The only things that had changed were the

PREFACE

outcomes: instead of looking to be big man/woman on campus and graduate, now people wanted titles, money, and promotions.

Just as in college, I was regularly pulled aside to talk about these challenges. Each time, I would wonder, often aloud, what we were doing to people that after all their education, they still didn't have the tools to know who they even were. What are we doing in business, that, in the name of success, people have chosen to "widgetize" themselves to fit the corporate model of success, not even knowing if it is what they really want? It is craziness!

We, as a society, have built these great institutions of education and industry to seemingly ingrain the greatest bottleneck for people: not knowing themselves. Most of us showed up to the corporate game because someone said that we had to, and that it was the only way to be successful. So, sadly, and often against our truest desires, strengths, and humanity, we did so.

I always felt the disconnection and saw the sadness in the eyes of people walking by me in their daily marches to work. With the one-size-fits-all model of the corporate mindset, all the various suits, dresses, briefcases, handbags, and shoes, just looked like different versions of the same thing to me: conformation. And, I had succumbed to it, too. However, one day, as I walked the streets of Chicago on my way to my corporate job, I had the overwhelming sensation that I had become just a tiny dot in an endless army of drones, and everything changed.

Over the years I, too, had been impacted by the corporate mindset. But that day was my last one that I showed up for the corporate ball. My spirit, energy, and thinking shifted. From that moment on, every decision in my life has been made from a place of strength, joy, and freedom. I began to elevate my sense as a leader from within, driving from the natural talents and strengths I had always possessed.

I learned to breathe into all my successes, current and past. I recognized what being a five-foot, four-inch collegiate high jumper and spending fifteen years of my life jumping over my own head had taught me. When no one thought that I was even tall enough to be in the game, I was learning lessons about setting goals, overcoming adversity, and excelling against stereotypes and false expectations that continue to serve me to this day. I re-engaged with that same desire for people to see that they had choice by working to embody it in every aspect of how I lived and led. But this time, and thanks to Tomer and several lengthy and insightful conversations, I was able to do so with a clear perspective that the game of the corporate mindset was a sham. You can't shove people's humanity into a box and then expect them to rise and perform well. It is illogical. Everything about top competitive performers (e.g., athletes, dancers, chess players, and artists) shows us that each moment where top-level performance is achieved, it is done by ensuring our whole selves are present. So it just became more logical to be a part of helping everyone take ownership of their leadership journey and join them as they became fully self-actualized, so they could bring their whole selves to the game. I figure that by doing so, we can beat the game—together.

Monika Black

Tomer's Preface

For much of my life, I was considered by others to be cynical, and often even depressed. My own mother, a clinical psychologist, believed that I suffered from dysthymia, a low-grade depression. In college, my small cohort of friends and I were often referred to as "the bitter old men," and just weeks into my first job out of college, at the ripe old age of twenty-one, a coworker told me I was "the kind of angry that only people over forty are allowed to be."

A lot of my upbringing minimized the positives that I liked about myself, as well as the accomplishments that I had achieved over the years as a classically trained pianist, athlete, and budding tech geek. It took me a lot of work, introspection, meditation, and therapy to authentically separate what was what. I came to realize that some of this cynicism was just authentically who I was. Other parts weren't so authentic. As it turns out, I have low vitamin D, so that was a primary driver behind the perceptions of melancholy. Other stuff was just what other people put on me. I am in a continuous process of evaluating what I learned from my life and what I want to keep, give back, or throw away. What has been left over for me to sort through has become quite an interesting collection.

A lot of these negative monikers that were applied to me weren't because I was bad or mean or even negative. Instead, what I've come to realize is that even at a young age, I had a pretty accurate understanding of what I was seeing out in the "real world," and, put simply, I disliked it. I would watch as I achieved, getting good grades, doing everything that was asked of me, and the rewards for doing so didn't seem to regularly come back to me as promised—at least, not enough. As I got further along in life, this only became truer. It seemed that no matter how well I performed, the rewards of raises, promotions, and accolades would fall to those who simply marketed themselves better. Thankfully, I discovered entrepreneurship at a fairly young age, launching my first business while still in college. It wasn't until years later that I realized my draw to being an entrepreneur was deeply tied to my aversion to corporate life and thinking. I desperately did not want to be a cog, especially not in someone else's system. I didn't have this language at the time, and only found productive expression of it after meeting Monika. But it was a burning truth that I always knew, even if I couldn't express it in words.

This led me down a long, joyful path of entrepreneurial ventures and launchings of ideas and working to turn them into businesses—fourteen in all. What I learned during this journey was that the value of ideas or people wasn't in their ability to cover all bases, but rather could they do one thing, maybe two, exceedingly well. This I could do. This gave me real engagement with my life and my strengths. This was the path to success. Whenever I looked up to see who was truly achieving in life, business, or anything else, it always came back to this truth: be INCREDIBLE at one thing and then, if you want, branch out from there.

Many people misinterpret this thinking to say you should be a great doctor or lawyer, and that the "one thing" is an occupation. For some, it can be, but that is rare. For the rest of us, that one thing is being ourselves. As the saying goes, nobody can be you better than you. Maybe that's your one thing, and maybe it is already more than enough.

Tomer Yogev

TandemSpring's Preface

In 2009, we met online and became partners in life and in business (thanks, match.com!). As we both shared, we have experienced the downside of the corporate mindset in our own lives and careers, and it was a point on which we immediately connected. Monika brought her strengths-based approaches, and Tomer brought his disdain for the corporate mindset. Together, we launched TandemSpring, became coaches, and, after watching our friends and colleagues suffer in the day-to-day humdrum of the corporate mindset, we developed a process for all people to unlock and become authentic leaders.

In that time, we have worked with leaders at all levels of organizations, big and small; with entrepreneurs; and across various community settings. We find that too many strong and positive leaders are sitting at the brink of leadership waiting "until they are ready" because at some point along the way they were taught that they must wait until they look the part, have a certain number of years under their belt, become recognized, etc. At the same time, so many people complain about working for people who are in positions of leadership not because of their leadership qualities or expertise, but because they toe the line—and in their organization, that is called leadership. Further, these so-called leaders, who have been promoted to their positions of power, feel they, too, are masquerading at the corporate ball. They complain of having to lead in positions that are not aligned with their strengths and true passions, and so even they suffer.

When we created TandemSpring in 2010, it was in the hopes of spreading a more whole and complete model of leadership. We combined our own individual consulting practices into TandemSpring because we felt everyone deserved a true partner in the journey to becoming their most authentic and brilliant selves. This book is no different in its intent. We want EVERYONE to know that the shortest path to the future they are hoping for is through identifying and leveraging their own strengths. By being authentically themselves, they already have everything they need, no matter what anyone else might think or say.

UNLOCK THE CORPORATE MINDSET

So, this book is for everyone who, like us, had a long, winding journey to figuring out who they really wanted to be when they grew up. For everyone who has ever thought that "there must be a better way." For all who ever doubted themselves and judged their abilities under the impossible framework that is put out there as the path to success. This is for those who ever felt that they had to apologize for not nailing every single step along the pathway of straight A's to graduating *summa cum laude* from Harvard to then becoming a Fortune 500 CEO. We were thinking of you whenever we found ourselves feverishly working on this book.

We genuinely believe that real answers to a great number of problems that many people wrestle with lie within these pages. With this book, you will be armed with the tools to change your current reality, become more of who you were always meant to be, and find a truly soul inspiring model of success that works for you! We hope that our perspective has a positive impact on you, and that as a result you present a more authentic sense of leadership to the world.

LET'S GET STARTED

> **THERE IS NO PASSION TO BE FOUND PLAYING SMALL, IN SETTLING FOR A LIFE THAT IS LESS THAN THE ONE YOU ARE CAPABLE OF LIVING.**
>
> —NELSON MANDELA

These inspirational words, from one of the most iconic individuals in our shared time in history, go right to the heart of everything we will try to convey in this book. While they seem simple, only a very select few live lives fully in the exploration of these words. For these rare people, this book should serve as a refresher. For the other 99.9% of us, this book's very purpose is to help you—through anecdotes, exercises, and sharing of what we have learned as executive coaches—to no longer settle for playing small and find your path to living the life you are capable of living.

Let us just put this as simply as we can:

You are worth more, and deserving of better, than the suffering you currently tolerate inside of the corporate mindset.

If you find this statement to be acknowledging of your daily struggle, we strongly encourage you to keep reading. If, instead, you found yourself a bit defensive, likely because you have an impressive-sounding title at work and/or a healthy salary, then we also ask that you keep reading. Either way, this book is totally designed for you, to redesign and improve your relationship with your job, your career, and your life, from the inside out. If, on the other hand, you are feeling us on what we're saying so far, but terrified for what it means for you, don't worry. We got you.

Unlocking the corporate mindset is about reevaluating, not beating people up for having been a part of the industrial complex, also known as "the machine" or "the matrix." We want you to realize your "why" for working for the machine and better understand your relationship with it, so you can consciously choose to engage from

LET'S GET STARTED

a place that makes you whole. As we go through the steps in this book, do not be surprised to discover that you have been 100 right all along—something isn't right in corporate life. Maybe you'll just want to make a few tweaks to maximize your capacity and to bring everything you have to the table. Perhaps you'll realize that you don't have to settle, and you can still go after your dream, maybe start your own business, or pursue a passion. You might just up and move to another country to start all over. The answer is not in these pages—only the path to find out for yourself.

The key to this work is that all your strengths, knowledge, and life experiences are designed for you to lead. The right role, the right context, the right alignment with your passion, all will allow you to lead well. You leading well, from your truest of strengths, will ensure you have a meaningful impact on the world around you. You will be free to engage as you see fit, able to hold yourself accountable for meaningful engagement in your work, and inspirational in how you work as you lead and live through your personal strengths. Unshackled by the corporate mindset, you are a free agent. No longer beholden to a degree, a boss, a career, or an organization, you sell your talents and skills to whomever you want. You are only beholden to yourself. You focus on the positive impact that you have on the people you care about, your community, and the world around you. And, if by leading well, you end up working for organizations, large or small, that are a good fit for you and your strengths, then all the better for everyone.

Within the lens of the corporate mindset that so many of us have adopted, even the paths to success seem rather awful. So, if you are feeling a bit of angst about next steps, or if you are thinking of the old adage "one step back to take two steps forward", please know that the journey out of the corporate mindset does not have to be filled with deficits and failure. We are given frameworks like the one below that set us up for some long, grueling tumbles into living and leading a better life.

UNLOCK THE CORPORATE MINDSET

The emotional journey of creating anything great
(according to some people)

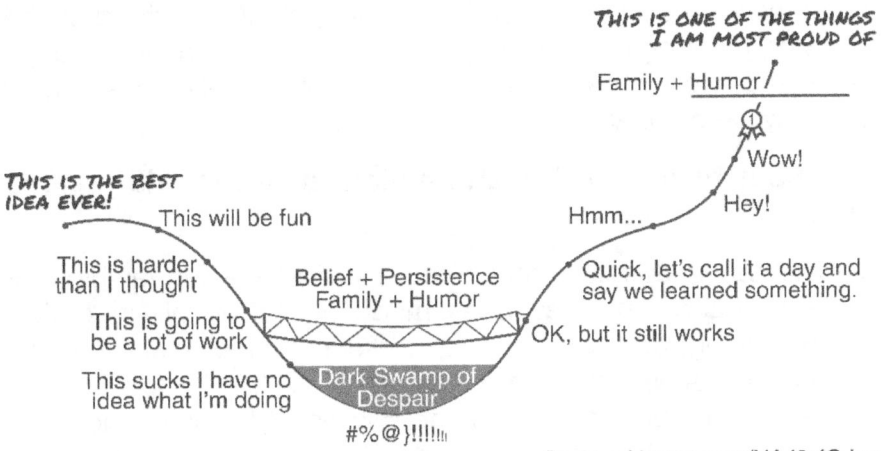

Source: i.imgur.com/UAJ2zjG.jpg

In this strange world, things get worse and worse until we reach the "dark swamp of despair" and then mysteriously, once we get over that rickety bridge of our beliefs, the climb to success is an unstoppable upward journey. But please remember, that this is only the "Emotional Journey of Creating Anything Great" from within the lens of the corporate mindset.

So how in organizations that promote leadership through followership are the "leaders" and the "employees" ever to find meaningful opportunities to realize their actual leadership potential? The reality is that they can't, and they aren't. That's why so many people feel that they are banging their heads against the corporate wall.

What if it simply does not have to be like that?! What if, for just a moment, we leave the "road to success is a hard path to follow" mentality and, in its place, turn inward, focus on ourselves, and realize that everything we need is already inside of us? From this vantage point, we can see that manifesting success is up to each one of us as individuals. That the successes and failures may just be rails along the journey of life to help keep us on track. That, in reality, very little in life is linear and instead much of it is cyclical.

LET'S GET STARTED

For these reasons, we have set upon a journey to unleash the strengths from within everyone so they can authentically rock their strengths and reach their true leadership potential. Guided by the following three core principles, we work to provide a lens through which each person can navigate the process of defining, stepping away, awakening, and overhauling the corporate mindset.

The path to radical transformation is paved with simple truths

Sometimes, things just aren't that hard. Take leadership, for example. Leadership has been made out to be this incredibly complex thing, mostly in an effort to keep everyone who has not been bestowed with the title of "leader" busy. It is not to say that a leader who jumped through all the corporate hoops cannot be a good leader, but rather to say that the person who hasn't can certainly be a leader, too. Leadership wonks continue to debate whether leadership is innate or taught. Why can't it just be both, and we leave it at that? The simple truth is that everyone has strengths, and those strengths can be mastered over time. If that is true, then leadership is innate and learned, practiced and mastered. It follows, then, that everyone is designed to lead in some meaningful way. We just have to look behind and around the title to see what people's true strengths are to understand their full leadership potential. In all, it's pretty simple; we've just chosen to make it hard.

Authentic leaders are led by their collective impact, not their ego

When authentic leaders become self-actualized and can operate fully in their leadership potential, there is a natural evolution to lead on behalf of others. Authentic leadership is not about title or salary or how big the P&L is that you are responsible for. Those are simple metrics designed to reward the ego. Authentic leadership is about the impact that one is able to have in the world. That impact can occur regardless of title. It can impact a few but carry great depth. It can shift the thinking of a large group of people. It can be a way of living that in its simplicity inspires others to live more peacefully. But the key is, leadership is inherently about others.

Leadership exists to inspire others beyond their own limitations; until you have done so, you have not truly led

There is a personal accountability—and therefore, responsibility—to lead so well that others are inspired to move beyond the forces that limit them. The great thing is, when we lead well, we automatically inspire people in the right way and for all the right reasons. Authentic leaders won't necessarily get a better title or money for leading well. But they will receive intimate moments of gratitude, texts, emails, cards, and community awards for inspiring others to find, live into, and elevate their true selves. What recognition they do inspire won't be through self-promotion. Rather, their community will provide them with continued opportunities to share their experiences so they can continue to elevate others.

So, before we officially embark on this journey together, let's go over the process. The key to this kind of change, like any kind of change, is that it comes in three parts: (1) recognize the situation, (2) figure out what you want to do about it, and then, 3) do it. So, in that same vein, we've laid out this book in three primary parts:

- First, "The Corporate Mindset" will help you to understand and identify the corporate mindset so you can more clearly see what role you might want to have in it.

- Next, "Unleashing From The Corporate Mindset And The Linear Illusion Of Success" will help you to understand how the corporate mindset has led to a faulty model of success and how you can devise your personal plan to change your role within and/or outside of the corporate mindset and become your own unique version of an authentic leader.

- Finally, "The Evolution To Radical Leadership", will provide you with a step-by-step process to help you to execute against your plan, provide accountability to yourself, and ensure you get to the kind of life that fully leverages your strengths and best serves you, your loved ones, your community, and the world.

With the right lens, real success can be much more positive, and fueled by your strengths and how you leverage them to become a leader in your own right, measured by your own definition of

LET'S GET STARTED

success in becoming a better you. The so-called setbacks, twists, turns, and "swamps of despair" can all be used to inform a better you, might just be there for all the right reasons, and aren't just crap you have to endure to become "great." Instead, we propose a model of success like the one on the next page (go ahead and take a peek, we'll wait right here).

If it looks more complicated, that's because it is. But, as we identify the corporate mindset, discover our ideal role inside of or alongside it, and take steps to become authentically ourselves, this chart will not only make more sense, but serve as a continuous guide for our self-discovery and our unlocking from the corporate mindset.

So, with that, we welcome you to the starting line of unlocking yourself from the corporate mindset and shifting toward the brighter side of leadership. Your journey will be informed by you, but the path is empowered by all of us. And, if you ever need a helping hand, we'll be there to jump right in alongside you.

Let's go!

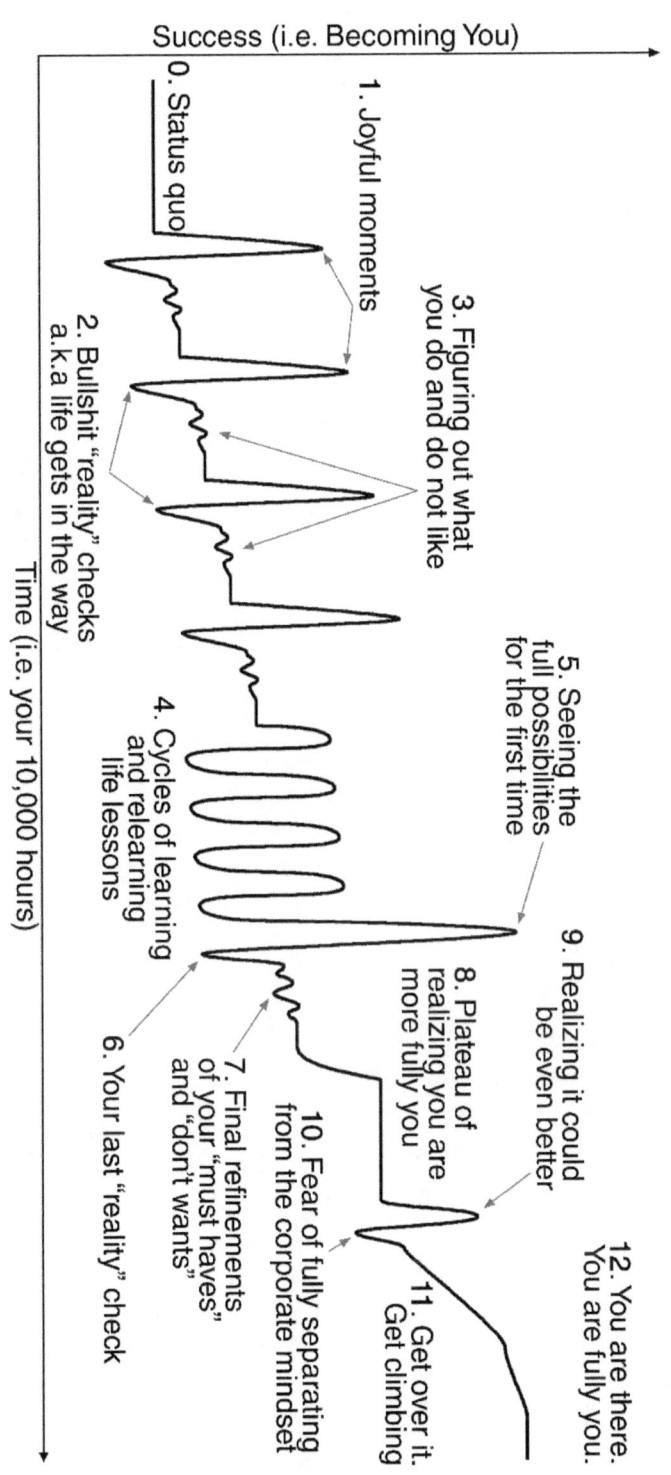

THE CORPORATE MINDSET

> "FITTING IN" OFTEN MEANS SHAVING OFF YOUR UNIQUE EDGES, HIDING AND MASKING WHAT DEFINES YOU, DISCARDING ANY BEHAVIORS OR APPEARANCES OR IMAGES THAT PROMPT OTHERS TO QUESTION YOU OR PUSH AWAY FROM YOU.
>
> —CHRIS BROGAN

We've all seen it. We've all been there. We know it and we feel it, sometimes subtly deep down, and sometimes so potent that, like a stinking onion, it can bring tears to our eyes. Some of us choose to choke it down and try to ignore it. Others are just left overwhelmed and don't know what to do. Some rebel, others flee. It is the corporate mindset.

At some point between the first time you ever set foot in a workplace as an employee and the moment you cracked open this book, you almost certainly noticed something was terribly wrong. As kids, we're all given similar hype and buildup about getting an education so you can get a good job, and from there work your way up the ladder and have a successful life. All of it, everything you were told to subscribe to, and perhaps forced to align with, now just seems very, very wrong.

Let us be clear: You are not crazy. In fact, you are exactly right!

It is a system built on lies and sustained by fear. But the good news is that you don't have to be party to it. Moreover, you can choose to operate completely outside of it or to subvert it while remaining inside. The key is, at the end of the day, to find your own truth, operate in that, and let the universe do the rest. Don't play the game. Beat the game.

> *"Only 33 percent of US workers are engaged."*
> *—Gallup*

THE CORPORATE MINDSET

According to The Engagement Institute, disengaged employees cost organizations between $450 and $550 billion annually. In our work as coaches, we have found that across CEOs, executive directors, mid-level managers, staff, lifers, and even the newest team members, very few are happy in their work. The corporate mindset is destructive to us as individuals, as teams, as companies, as industries, and even to society as a whole. The dance of the corporate ball requires us to put on a mask to fit in, instead of embracing our unique differences to drive new thinking and innovation. It benefits the seldom few, not just those at the "top," as we are often led to believe. It refuses the opportunity for individual self-expression, self-realization, joy, and, perhaps most important, the application of true wisdom, creativity, and innovation.

We are going to spend our first few pages together working to clearly define the corporate mindset. This will help us to see the veil behind which it continuously hides and operates. From there, and, to the extent it is not working for you, we can consciously decide to begin our journey moving away from the corporate mindset and its effects. Later, we will show you how you can join us to tear down these rules so all people can build their own games, with their own rules, in ways that make them stronger and more successful. There is a whole world of joy, opportunity, and success, far greater than what the horribly flawed rules of the corporate mindset have to offer; we just have to find our way there. And like any journey, the first step is understanding where you are.

What is the Corporate Mindset?

Often, we get asked, "What exactly *IS* the corporate mindset?"

Like asking, "What is art?" the corporate mindset is somewhat difficult to define, but oh so obvious when you see and experience it. It is the unspoken rules of the workplace environment that reinforce the illusion of a linear path to success and validate the hierarchy of power that, in turn, sets the tone, energy, and business practices that drive organizations. Now, that's a mouthful, but let's break it down a bit. It is the corporate mindset that leads to "yes men" and employee disengagement. It is the corporate mindset that seeps beyond the business world and into how we consume goods and media. It informs our half-true rules of thumb like "Get a degree, get a job, get money, and you'll be successful," and "Work hard, play hard."

Further, and perhaps most damning, is that the corporate mindset must, for its own survival, keep most people from becoming leaders. We often get pushback on this one, as those who buy into the corporate mindset most deeply feel that it does everything it can to promote people to leadership. We disagree, and we'll prove just how untrue that perception really is.

What if there was a phrase so common that literally everyone has heard it, and most of us have even used it? What if it perfectly illuminated the corporate mindset's need to keep a balance between leaders and non-leaders, often forcing people from ever trying to elevate into leadership while inspiring complacency in non-leadership roles? And, just for good measure, what if this same phrase showed its age and uselessness by leveraging dated racialized stereotypes?

"Too many chiefs, not enough Indians."

Remember this golden oldie? Sure you do! It is a near-perfect single-sentence embodiment of the corporate mindset in action. First, it is a great example of the systemic racism that we have

THE CORPORATE MINDSET

embedded in our everyday speech and ways of thinking about leadership, but that's for another book. Second, deconstructing the message, we believe that there are plenty of situations where there are too many leaders and not enough doers. Situations where we need to limit the number of voices heard in the name of getting something done efficiently and effectively.

The corporate mindset has done such a phenomenal job of inundating us with messages like this that many of us have come to believe that there are, in fact, situations where there are too many leaders and, by proxy, we then question the legitimacy of our own leadership potential. Even those already in top leadership positions regularly question if they are cut out for the task. Why? Perhaps because most of us, at some point earlier on in our careers, likely as a justification for why we, as less-experienced entrants in the workforce, had to do some incredibly menial tasks and not have our thoughts listened to, were told we were followers and not leaders.

Looking back, it is clear that in most cases this was told to you more out of fear of having to actually deal with your abilities than what was actually best for you, the team, or the company. Likely, that annoyed and frustrated reaction you had to being told to sit your ass down and just do your job, was, in fact, an early telltale sign of how the corporate mindset reinforces itself by maintaining the status quo. But, like most of us, you were probably not aware of all this at the time, so you grumbled to yourself and did as you were told. And this was encouraged. You were growing up and learning how the real world works. And, for those rare few who didn't comply, you probably know what comes next: some kind of disciplinary action or just jump straight to being fired, also known as removing you before "one bad apple spoils the bunch."

So, what is behind all this? Some call it "the man." The more conspiracy-theory-oriented among us might call it the "Illuminati" or, more recently, "the one percenters." Most of us seem to just be itching to lay the responsibility for this structure at the feet of a single entity, be it our boss or company's CEO. Effectively, we place blame on the highly "successful" (i.e., rich), as certainly they must be behind all this. Certainly, it seems that they are the ones who benefit, so it follows that they would be the ones to actively reinforce this kind of thinking for their own personal—often financial—benefit.

But, as we spent more time with the people who, as leaders, imposed the corporate mindset within their own organizations, it became immediately apparent that while they certainly benefit from this structure financially, they are just as damaged by it emotionally and psychologically. Do not lose sight of the fact that to get to where they are, they, too, had to play the same games and drink the same Kool-Aid you are finding so distasteful. Moreover, for them to reach the top, they probably had to do all that for incredibly long periods of time, making it that much more crushing for them to find out that it is really no better at the top than it was when they were on the bottom. Even those leaders who are actively aware of their unhappiness in the corporate mindset, and desperately want to shift from it, are often so paralyzed by their own fear of change and having to address their role in all of it that they never do. So instead, they dig their heels in deeper and fall back on adages like "No pain, no gain," and other corporate mindset half-truths.

All of that said, the corporate mindset is quickly becoming obsolete. It is driving a perpetual system of fear, ego-driven power, and rampant unhappiness across every level of the corporate structure. Increasingly, it can no longer bear its own weight.

It was one thing when this form of business leadership was first developed in the early days of the industrial revolution. People worked hourly shifts along assembly lines, and so forth. It wasn't perfect, but it made a certain degree of sense. You needed people to work the line and only a select few to supervise and make sure things flowed smoothly. But in today's brain-based economy, where success is determined by your ingenuity, speed to market, and ability to grow, the old rules simply no longer apply. Today's economy is driven by innovative thought, and that can come from anywhere and anybody. So regardless of how we may define the word, how can one attain success? Well, clearly it isn't going to be by following rules that were never meant to let you win!

THE CORPORATE MINDSET

Let's start with a couple of ground rules. You're going to want to really get these before we move on to the deeper stuff:

- Regardless of title, EVERYONE has strengths and talents that can be effectively leveraged inside and outside of the business world.

- If we all have strengths and talents, then nobody should have to feel compelled to tolerate that which is at the root of their unhappiness just in the name of getting a paycheck.

- The bottom line is that organizational cultures and the corporate world would all benefit if they could just operate differently and actually unleash, rather than stymie, the strengths of all people to do what they do best.

Simple enough, right? Yet at just about any organization you encounter, these truths are, at best, talking points—and at worst, actively ignored.

Deep down, we all know that the corporate mindset and the rule set it reinforces just don't work. Moreover, the further separated we are from being a wealthy Christian heterosexual able-bodied cis-gendered white male, the less applicable any of these rules and expectations are to us. However, it seems that to function in the workplace we all must learn to swallow these "truths" and step in line with the corporate mindset in the name of earning a paycheck and being a good employee. The game is so deeply woven into our social fabric and our individual survival mentality that to even question the corporate mindset, let alone turn our backs on it, feels like a crazy risk, even when it is the only thing that might ever make us whole.

We spend a lot of time in our society and in this book talking about leadership and being a leader. But few have ever stopped to consider what those terms really mean and exactly how far they reach. People often debate what is leadership and who is a leader/follower. We posit that everyone is a leader, designed to inspire others beyond their own limitations. Each person is designed to lead at what they are naturally talented and "studied" in. For you that could mean soccer coach, and for me it could mean chef and restaurant owner. It is our talents that we have turned into

UNLOCK THE CORPORATE MINDSET

strengths that tell us how we lead. Further, it is our unique combination of strengths, passions, and desired impact that tells us what we are designed to best lead at. If we are all leaders at what we are best at, then we are all followers at what others are best at. We all lead. We all follow. When and where we lead and follow will vary by goal, context, strengths, and the talents of others. So to be clear, when we use the term "leader," the typical interpretation of a business CEO, a military general, or president of a country is only a tiny segment of the context we are referring to. You are a leader, right now, even if you haven't realized it yet.

"We're here for a reason. I believe a bit of the reason is to throw little torches out to lead people through the dark."
—Whoopi Goldberg

At the end of the day, leadership has less to do with how far up a corporate ladder you can climb and far more to do with how well you can live within your authentic self and be the real version of you, allowing others to follow in your model of authenticity and, in turn, become leaders of their own. So, to hell with the corporate mindset! Join us on the brighter side of leadership!

THE CORPORATE MINDSET

The shift from the corporate mindset to the brighter side of leadership

Corporate Mindset	On The Brighter Side of Leadership
Leadership is top down.	Everyone is a leader and can lead from where they are.
There is little room at the top for leaders.	There is plenty of room at the top for all leaders.
Good employees fit into the culture of the organization.	Good organizations build a culture that fits all of their leaders.
Employees are to toe the company line.	Leaders are to challenge the status quo.
Employees are to fit into the corporate culture.	Leaders are to bring their whole selves to work.
Fear and stress are good motivators for performance.	Leading through strengths inspires everyone to higher levels of performance.
Conflict is a problem.	Conflict is an opportunity.
Diversity is a burden.	Diversity is a strength.

We are living in a wonderfully complex time, where we can revolutionize that portion of our lives spent being unhappy with our jobs, and instead do what we love, what we do best, with meaning, engagement, and impact. As shown in the chart above, this is what we call the brighter side of leadership. It doesn't matter if you never worked a day in your life or if you are a veteran CEO. You can make this change. You just need the strength and confidence to start thinking like a leader on the brighter side of leadership.

UNLOCK THE CORPORATE MINDSET

How leaders think on the brighter side of leadership

- The deficit-oriented thinking of the corporate mindset is a costly and less efficient way to lead.

- Embracing my strengths with passion, purpose, and a little bit of strategy is a far more effective way to lead.

- Elevating the strengths of others is a much more productive model of leadership than focusing on weaknesses.

- Given time (see Malcolm Gladwell's theory about 10,000 hours) and opportunity to meaningfully apply strengths to an area of passion, anyone can turn talents into strengths and become an authentic leader.

- Focusing on strengths begets more strengths, which is a much more fun and productive way of leading that can yield greater positive returns with a radiating positive impact for others (e.g., clients, partners, family, community, and the world).

Knowing The Corporate Mindset When You See It

The first step in ridding ourselves of the corporate mindset is to know it when we encounter it. While we've previously defined the corporate mindset, it is important to recognize that it is so imbued into our cultural and societal norms, we often mistake it for "just the way the world works." Beyond that, most of us have picked up so many bad habits that stem from subscribing to the corporate mindset, we need to actively change what we do and how we do it just to see the corporate mindset at work.

When it comes to the ways in which so many of us live and work, we have a lot of it wrong. The kicker is that we know it. Yet we put on our masks and show up for the dance anyway. Allow us to explain: How many people do you know (and perhaps this even applies to you) wake up and seem to turn on the same old music, knowing it is not their song? They sign up for the same old corporate line dance, hoping something different will come out of it. They "fake it" but in all likelihood, they'll never "make it." It is the masquerade of the corporate ball. Daunting, but also very real for a lot of people who are not engaged in life and work in a way that is truly meaningful for them.

> *The way we're working isn't working.*
> *—The Energy Project (2014)*

The Energy Project shined some much-needed light on our collective dirty secret: most of us hate our jobs. The good news, however, is that the problem is not with you! It is just the way our systems and processes have been established and continue to operate in the modern working world. The Energy Project article points out a myriad of factors that workplaces do not allow for in what they call the "White-Collar Salt Mine."

UNLOCK THE CORPORATE MINDSET

Key factors lacking in the workplace

- Regular time for creative or strategic thinking (70 percent do not have this at work)

- Ability to focus on one thing at a time (66 percent do not have this at work)

- Opportunities to do what is most enjoyed (60 percent do not have this at work)

- Level of meaning and significance (50 percent do not have this at work)

- Connection to company's mission (50 percent do not have this at work)

- A sense of community (49 percent do not have this at work)

Their list goes on, but to this list, we would also like to add that most workplaces also do not allow for:

- Honest joyful moments and celebrations of life's successes

    Not every moment needs to include jumping up and down with joy. But even the moments specifically designed to be joyous within the corporate mindset end up being these painful and depressing affairs. Think of the half-hearted birthday song most business teams sing over store-bought half-frozen cake. Do your joyful moments at work resemble the birthday cake scene from *Office Space*? If you're not familiar with it, look it up on YouTube—just Google "Office Space Happy Birthday"—it's a perfect reenactment of something we've all lived through.

- Strengths-based ways of thinking and being

    Are you asked to do tasks because you are actually good at them or just because someone needs to do them and they more or less just fell to you? Do people at your workplace even know what their strengths are, let alone operate in them regularly, let alone know your strengths? Is work aligned with the person, or does the person have to conform to the work and its rules and regulations?

THE CORPORATE MINDSET

- A model of leadership that advances you into being the leader you want to be

When was the last time someone at work really wanted to learn what you wanted to do with your life?

Unfortunately, this rings true for most places that we and our business partners have worked. We have seen it all: abusive leadership, inhumane actions, and even downright illegal behavior. All of this stifles the workplace environment and dampens, if not crushes, any chance at employee engagement.

Not too surprisingly, this is also how and why we ended up working for ourselves. We decided long ago that we were D-O-N-E with the corporate bullshit. We don't want that nonsense for ourselves, and we don't want it for you. So let's stop masquerading.

Checklist for masquerading at the corporate ball

☐ You wince at the thought of going into work each morning. But you still put on the clothes and makeup, do your hair, and get out there and do it, in spite of yourself.

☐ You somehow find yourself sitting at your desk each morning, coffee in hand, but you may not really remember how you got there, let alone why you're really there.

☐ You find that you have already disengaged from various meetings before you even show up because you know that nothing is really going to get accomplished . . . again.

☐ You have a side-hustle that no one at work knows about. You sneak time and energy at work thinking about and planning how you are going to do more of that because it is what really makes you happy.

☐ There is a big disconnect between "weekend you" and "weekday you" because you have bottled up all your freaky goodness and shoved it into a suit Monday through Friday.

☐ You find yourself exhausted at the end of the day from the performance that you have been putting on for the past eight to nine hours.

UNLOCK THE CORPORATE MINDSET

If you nodded in agreement to even one of these, the next obvious question is, how do you stop masquerading? We'll explore that in the next section. But take a moment to consider what it would look like if you didn't masquerade and we didn't have to operate in the corporate mindset. Or put differently, what if rather than the old workplace adage of "Shit rolls downhill," there was no "shit" and there wasn't even a "hill"?

Take Your "Shit" and Take Your "Hill" and Just Leave Us Alone!

Think of the oh-so-common workplace phrase "Shit rolls downhill." Which, for those who may be unfamiliar with it, simply means that the lowest ranking person in an organization nearly always gets stuck doing the task nobody wants to do. First off, can we just take a moment to acknowledge what an incredibly ridiculous deficit-oriented concept this is?! Second, how is it that we use this as a workplace truism?

But let's also take a moment to dismantle this seemingly innocuous phrase: "shit" clearly refers to some undesirable thing, and in this case usually a task, project, or other responsibility that nobody wants to claim. Then, we have the idea of "downhill," which clearly references a workplace hierarchy where the person at the bottom has the least power and authority, and, by proxy, the least-valued thoughts, skills, and strengths. We're not even going to get into how the shit, as it rolls downhill like a cartoon snowball, picks up other shit and grows to be an immense ball of crap. Instead, let's just ask ourselves what if there wasn't any "shit"? What if there wasn't a "downhill" because there was never a hill in the first place?

It is worth noting here, this is what the "entitled" and "whiny" millennial population is calling forward. And, thank goodness, because none of us really liked it anyway!

Rather than forcing a task on someone, we might instead take a brief pause and look to align the task with a team member's strengths and/or interests. Instead of this responsibility rolling in any predetermined direction, what if there was some thought put not only into who is well-suited to succeed, but who could actually benefit, learn, and maybe even take joy from accomplishing this task? That person could possibly come to see the task as an opportunity to hone their strengths and develop into an even more valuable member to the team and organization. The best part is that the extra time it might take to figure this out will, in the end, cost the organization far less than the combined costs of the task being done half-assed, the inevitable negative effects on the person on whom it landed and who is forced to do it, and the ongoing costs of maintaining an organization in spite of such a strong hierarchy and general workplace unpleasantness in the first place.

But if there is no "shit" and no "hill," what's left?

Several years ago, a colleague who had been trying to clean out her library gave us the book *Empowerment for High Performing Organizations*, written by Phil Guillory and Linda Galindo. It transitioned from our colleague's library to ours, where it continued to collect dust for a few months. Finally, out of our own personal fear of becoming like our colleague and having to clean out an entire library of books, we were inspired to action; so one Sunday morning, the book was finally cracked open. By the end of chapter one, one of the finest formulas for business success had already been laid out before us.

It rang through with simple brilliance: when an individual and the team are truly empowered and supported with organizational systems and resources, the entire organization becomes empowered. Now, to be sure, "empowered" is one of those business words used so often it has come to mean almost nothing. But here, Guillory and Galindo have established empowerment as the very foundation for a high-performing organization. It isn't just some leadership buzzword; it is the very crux of building success.

This may not sound like rocket science, and many might look at this as a simple matter of fact. But the key to the model is subtler and deeply profound: It demands transformation at the individual level. It forces each and every person within the organization to be clear in their personal beliefs and responsibilities in the name of being empowered. Beyond that, each person, to be empowered, must also have the freedom and resources to consistently act, with full accountability to their beliefs and responsibilities.

Which brings us to accountability—the engine behind operating in one's strengths and the key to stopping the masquerade. It is only

THE CORPORATE MINDSET

through accountability to self that we can achieve as individuals, teams, and organizations. Let's explore this with an example:

> Phil is an employee of a company and has strong beliefs about how things should get done, what quality work really looks like, etc. Further, he is clear on what he is good at and what he enjoys doing. When Phil is asked to complete a task, he has a choice: he can choose to view it from a deficit model and thereby slog through the task, or he can identify how it aligns with his strengths, beliefs, and responsibilities and hopefully find the task much easier to accomplish. This is all well and good. But where issues pop up is when Phil is unable to find alignment between the task and his strengths, beliefs, or responsibilities. This is where the corporate mindset encourages "strong management," which effectively means forcing Phil to do something he doesn't want to do. Clearly, over a long enough time horizon, this is not a sustainable model.
>
> Instead, if we empower Phil to leverage his personal truths, as well as his teammates', there almost certainly will be some other way to get the same task done. It may not look like we originally thought. It may not get done exactly as originally envisioned. But it is more than likely that the task will get done better, faster, and cheaper than it has ever been done before because it has transitioned from a chore that landed on poor Phil to a step in building upon someone's strengths, talents, and goals.

We can clearly see the corporate mindset at work here. It is through leveraging our strengths, finding our truths, empowering ourselves, and becoming accountable to ourselves that we can most immediately replace this mindset with a new way modality that is far more enjoyable, effective, and profitable for all parties. Unleash from the corporate mindset so that we can all do epic shit!

Don't take shit. Do epic shit!

In the corporate mindset, the logical response to a challenge of any sort is to grind through it and find some other way to achieve happiness and meaning in life. Grind through the project. Grind

UNLOCK THE CORPORATE MINDSET

through the job that you don't even want but you took because someone told you that you couldn't make enough money doing what you really wanted to do. Take the promotion even though it is more of doing the same, at the same job that you never really liked. Grind through the commute. The list goes on and on. And this is the reality that so many people live: in the grind of the corporate mindset, just hoping to find some work-life balance in their free time.

On the brighter side of leadership, there is little need for the day-to-day humdrum in pursuit of work-life balance. In fact, there is need for work-life balance only if work and life are different things. If both work and life are joyful expressions of self, then you don't have to worry about balancing them. Epic shit will get done. By simply being you, you will be leading well in business and in life. It's a crazy concept in the corporate mindset. But it is pretty simple on the brighter side of leadership.

If you now recognize the corporate mindset and are ready to find your way out of it, let's move on and move on up! In the next section, we will set the tone for you to begin to put the "you" back at the center of the equation and begin to comfortably move toward a different way of living and leading. This will put you on the path to finding your own manner of being, express it to the world, and find real joy in your work and in your life.

UNLEASHING FROM THE CORPORATE MINDSET AND THE LINEAR ILLUSION OF SUCCESS

> PRODUCTION BY MACHINE HAS LED TO A PECULIAR ILLUSION THAT THE ROAD TO EXCELLENCE IS STRAIGHT AND PLEASANT... THINKING IN THE INDUSTRIALIZED WORLD COVETS NO FAILURES AND KNOWS NO EXCELLENCE.
>
> —ERICH FROMM

From the previous section, we now know what the corporate mindset looks and feels like and are newly committed to doing some epic shit. In this section, we're going to start working on how to really do all that and how to get to a place where we are bringing our whole selves to our work and everything else we do.

Erich Fromm's *The Art of Loving* explores the disintegration of love in contemporary Western society. His view comes from the perspective of a society influenced by the industrial revolution and the subsequent disconnectedness that followed. As a result of the industrial revolution, mass production, and the resulting spike in consumption, a few key shifts happened in society:

- People moved to less-congested suburbs and disconnected from life in the city and the visual reminder that our lives are deeply connected.

- Labor became equated with following orders and toeing the company line.

- Power in the organization was transitioned to external investors who were defined by their drive for profits.

- The division of labor became much more extreme and individuals lower in rank became cogs in the machine.

- Success became defined by the ability to amass things and wield power, to the point that those who simply had more stuff were idolized, regardless of how they got there.

UNLEASHING FROM THE CORPORATE MINDSET AND THE LINEAR ILLUSION OF SUCCESS

Fromm's key point in highlighting these transitions was that the shift from the individual to bureaucracy did not foster greater independence, but instead a dependence on the system such that no one was truly free. Everyone became dependent on some form of bureaucracy, be it management or the systems created to fight management. Consequently, the automatization of the corporate ball was constantly reinforced as people felt compelled to sign up in the name of self-preservation. Duped into thinking they are free to choose and caught in their own "illusion of success," people would consciously choose to sign up for the corporate ball, not realizing they are already there. This is how people became drones in the corporate mindset.

We can't keep wondering why so few of us feel we are meaningfully engaged at work and not look at the very system that disconnected the self from the work. This gap in our collective consciousness has caused a whole series of workarounds, Band-Aids, and maladaptive behaviors that people subscribe to in the name of coping, job security, and playing the game in the corporate mindset that are completely unproductive.

The ways in which we try to take care of ourselves in the corporate mindset are proving insufficient to close the gap. In fact, that gap is widening as various forms of self-medication (e.g., alcohol, smoking, spending, watching TV, etc.) have normalized escapism from work, causing a whole series of other problems. So now when we are at work we are not engaged, and then we go home to disengage even further, in the name of unwinding so that we can have enough energy to wake up for another day at the corporate ball. Crazy, huh?! It is no wonder we have lost ourselves in the gap, so much so that it cripples our work, which is now impacting our personal lives and broader sense of agency in the world. There are myriad challenges and barriers we now have as a part of day-to-day life.

Challenges of day-to-day life in the disintegration of love

- We see each other as competition and not as collaborators.

- We are often disconnected from our true selves and therefore each other, and the masses feel misunderstood.

- We struggle to reconcile our own loss of humanity in the corporate mindset and therefore cannot have empathy for the loss of self that others feel.

- We dislike the restrictions placed upon us but don't mind the limitations placed on others, if it allows us to continue on or get ahead.

- We are no longer discomforted enough by lying, fraudulent actions, and/or criminal behavior to say or do anything about it, for fear of losing a job that isn't even serving us.

The corporate mindset sets the trap for self-imposed down-spiraling in the name of "climbing the corporate ladder." It then creates a blind spot to everything that we need to overcome the fears that hold us back from becoming whole. From the gap of disconnectedness, people continuously try to give their best and engage in ways that they hope will feel real and fulfilling. But if any of what has been introduced above is true, then people are unconsciously setting themselves up for their own failure. They do so in the name of achieving higher levels of success, despite the fact that the system has already ensured that they can't bring their whole selves to the table and therefore they won't be able to perform at their best. This does not even speak to the number of systemic biases that people have normalized over years in their understanding of who can be a leader and who is not a "good fit." So how can we continue to expect people to not bring their whole selves to work, and from there continue to do amazing things? We can't. Or at least we can't without significant repercussions.

We know that many people can feel their backs are already against the wall. This may take the form of not having enough time or finances, or other resource constraints. Alternatively, the "load" on them may feel too great. Too many mouths to feed, too many bills to pay, too many other responsibilities, and so on. Certainly, within

UNLEASHING FROM THE CORPORATE MINDSET AND THE LINEAR ILLUSION OF SUCCESS

such a context, a model such as the one we are proposing here may feel daunting, if not impossible. However, that is the voice of corporate mindset. We contend that it is exactly in these moments that switching to a new model shifts from a self-improvement opportunity to a self-preservation imperative. If the system isn't working for you, as evidenced by the overwhelming state of affairs, then you must play not to win but to beat the game altogether. Not doing so is, by far, the riskier option in a system that fights against the change that the everyday person needs to become empowered. Treading water might keep you alive for now, but it doesn't get you anywhere, and nobody can tread forever.

Having now explored the symptoms and effects of the corporate mindset, it seems ridiculous that it even still exists. However, what is particularly ironic is that the corporate mindset continues to exist despite the fact that it does such a terrible job of achieving its own stated goals. It exists in spite of itself. There is a mountain of evidence that the very outcomes the corporate mindset seeks to achieve (profits, effectiveness, efficiency, productivity, structure, etc.) are less likely to occur in environments run in such an overly regulated and hierarchical manner. So, we must find a different way of engaging to even achieve the very goals of the corporate mindset. Moreover, when we apply these rules to ourselves, as individuals, we clearly limit our ability to achieve. All the more reason why we need to break out. But the first step to doing that is knowing who we are and bringing that, in full, to everything we do.

Bringing Your Whole Self To Work

To bring your whole self to work, you must be able to forge a complete identity, such that your individuality can more fully exist within the collective and without compromise. This requires a complete sense of self first, and for all of the right reasons. So, it is not selfish to focus on self. You must focus on yourself so that you can be whole, and, in time, more selfless. Once you are whole, then your whole self can connect to other whole selves, at home, at work, in the broader community, and in society without any internal conflict or need for unproductive coping mechanisms. There will be no mask and no dance at the corporate ball, hence there will be no corporate mindset. There will simply be you.

The key to reintegrating your whole self is reconnecting with your moments of truth. To embrace the fullness of your strengths, and from there to create a more whole and complete sense of yourself, including all of your awesomeness. The fear that we are not enough and don't have what it takes are the negative thoughts that constantly hold us back from letting our truth be realized. But, we all had moments of awesomeness, when we were simply at our best. If you were awesome then, you must still have the capacity for awesomeness now. So naturally, you are more than ready to be successful at whatever you are designed to be the best at.

Productive engagement

If the corporate mindset is unproductive, then engaging through authenticity is productive. The challenge is that the corporate mindset has shamed people into an incomplete version of authenticity, such that it is hard to conceptualize what it means to be truly authentic anymore. One common example is the feeling that you can't really say what you want to say for fear that it will be seen as being "too much." So saying what you really want to say in the corporate mindset is regulated and evaluated through HR policies. Outside of the corporate mindset, you owning your truths and saying what you want to say can be illuminating and inspiring.

UNLEASHING FROM THE CORPORATE MINDSET AND THE LINEAR ILLUSION OF SUCCESS

Maybe even innovative. Let's walk through a simple everyday example that you probably have experienced.

You are facilitating a meeting and know that you are running out of time and need to cut the conversation short to get through the agenda. You might worry about how to do that in a way that won't offend people.

Corporate mindset says

"Everyone, I hate to do this, but we need to move along here."

On the brighter side of leadership says

"This is great conversation, and I want to acknowledge everything that people have shared. I also want to acknowledge that we are running out of time. If it is okay, I would like to pick up the pace so we can move along the agenda, but I also hope to create an opportunity for us to come back to this because I hear that it is important for us to talk about these things. Is that okay with everyone?"

Do you see the difference? Do you think the others in the room might feel a difference?

Productive engagement looks and sounds like saying everything that you really want to say so fully that you acknowledge your anxieties and concerns, as well as any challenges you feel others might be facing. Leading up and through authenticity could rarely be a problem for other people who are whole. It surfaces as conflict only for those who are locked in the corporate mindset and receive your truth as a threat and intimidation (e.g., "Who are you to speak to me like that?!"). Note that your authentic self might trigger those who are still buying into the corporate mindset because they still need to believe that the rules of the matrix ring true to justify their own behaviors in climbing up the corporate ladder. Real and authentic engagement affirms your truths and the truths of others while creating space and opportunity to have more engagement. In this way, the response to those who would otherwise feel threatened is simply to demonstrate that I am me, and you are you, so you are welcome to speak freely, too.

Acceptance to embrace

The corporate mindset breeds an unhealthy level of tolerance. The very definition of tolerance in the workplace is wrought with unproductive innuendo. Especially in light of the fact that we have weaponized the very concept of intolerance to equate with challenging the status quo, or insubordination. But when we look to leading negotiation and conflict resolution models, there are various methods by which we can navigate these situations that, while they may require more energy up front, are considerably more productive in achieving positive results in the longer term.

Outside of the corporate mindset, difference, challenging conversations, and conflict can all be incredibly productive. Disrupting the status quo is seen as a key to new learning and therefore driving innovation (e.g., this is true for organizations like Google that tend to foster environments that inspire positive conflict). In a more productive engagement environment, people have more space to bring their whole selves. This reinforces an acceptance of one's self and of others. The natural evolution of accepting one's self fosters acceptance of others and promotes a deeper understanding that, in turn, results in even further collaboration. Differences can be embraced in a whole new light. Differences can be defined by thoughts and ideas, behaviors, strengths, methodologies, culture, and a million other things to be turned into a vehicle for productive conversation, insight, and innovation.

Becoming a Productive Leader

In the corporate mindset, you spend eight-plus hours a day consumed with achieving success. The fact that you are focused on achieving success is not the problem. The problem is, whose definition of success are you so incredibly focused on? As mentioned above, capitalism has forced an external model of success, one dictated by the goals of the shareholder—or in the case of nonprofits, the board.

For most of us, our own personal life goals are not included, or even welcome, inside of the company's goals. All that work with which you spend so many hours trying to achieve success is often intentionally disconnected from your actual life goals. Remember that when you get home. Remember it when you take the much-needed time out of your personal life just to "wind down" and escape from the corporate mindset. You may also have family needs to meet. So, at the end of the day, how much time do you really have to achieve your goals in life, if your goals cannot be achieved within the organization you work at?

Key questions to ask yourself about being a productive leader:

- On a scale of 1–10, to what extent do you feel self-actualized?
- How much of your time in a particular day is spent on your life passions and goals?
- What percentage of your life passions and goals can be accomplished at and through your work?
- What percentage of your talents and strengths are you only using elsewhere in life, outside of work?

Now, consider Maslow's Hierarchy of Needs. For those unfamiliar, it is a model that states that we progress from physiological needs, to safety needs, to love/belongingness needs, to esteem needs, to self-actualization, and finally to transcendence. The last two stages are of particular interest, as this is when we become fully ourselves and then in transcendence are able to provide openly to others. There is much written about Maslow's Hierarchy of Needs, so if this model makes intuitive sense to you, you may want to explore it further. It aligns very neatly with the strengths-based approaches outlined in this book.

Maslow positions his hierarchy as a set of building blocks (the image most often used is that of a layered pyramid with each need neatly stacked atop the preceding need), but they are really more like a progression through a passageway that has the self as a critical final component of a forever-continuing process. For illustration, consider turning the traditional pyramidal model of Maslow's Hierarchy of Needs on its side with an arrow pointing to the right. That arrow is the self, but the path through the hierarchy tends to revolve and circumnavigate the self, resulting in what may appear to be a messy nonlinear progression. This we call the continuous evolution of you.

The continuous evolution of you

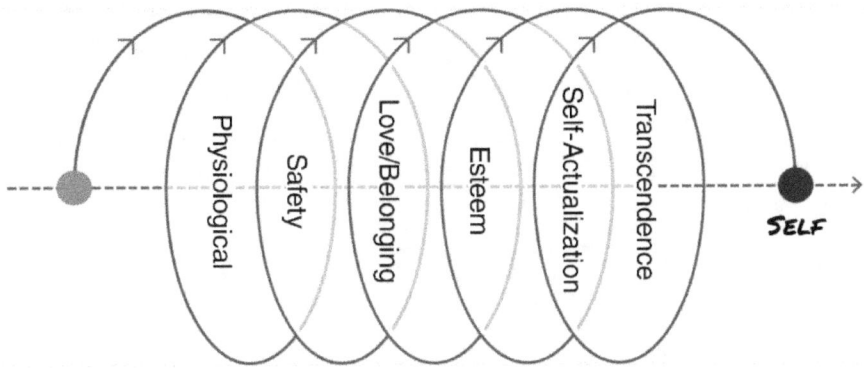

Most people can navigate through the first four stages of Maslow's hierarchy well enough. Most of us have food and shelter, are relatively safe, feel at least somewhat loved, and probably even think reasonably well of ourselves. If you can agree to at least that much, then you're probably good on the first four stages. However, to be sure, there are many people who struggle, for various personal, corporate mindset, and other reasons, to get to and/or sustain their physiological, safety, love/belongingness, and

UNLEASHING FROM THE CORPORATE MINDSET AND THE LINEAR ILLUSION OF SUCCESS

esteem needs. Self-actualization, the fifth stage, is where most modern people tend to get stuck. For whatever reason we find ourselves stuck at that phase, the reason why getting unstuck can be so difficult largely lies in the issues we've previously discussed: the corporate model for success and self-actualization put forth in our society is deeply flawed. The underlying assumptions are wrong. The rules of the linear model of success are not the rules, and the milestones along the path are not the right markers, at least not for most of us.

Of course, no model is exactly right for all people. But for those who are on a journey of living into their authentic selves, it is often a nonlinear trajectory, a cyclical and often wonderfully messy evolution. Done right, it continually drives toward one's truest self, actualization, and beyond that, transcendence, just as Maslow's model would suggest.

Defying The Linear Model of Success

Today there are plenty of examples of success being redefined outside traditional models, at both the individual and organizational levels. Some are well known, like Richard Branson of Virgin or Phil Knight of Nike, both capitals of industry who came from nowhere, or Malala Yousafzai, the youngest Nobel Prize laureate, or Anne Wojcicki, cofounder and CEO of 23andMe, which is blowing up the genetics and insurance markets, or the ladies behind the Black Lives Matter movement, Alicia Garza, Opal Tometi, and Patrisse Cullors, who have rocked the political landscape. Countless others are less well known but are every bit as significant, be it to their local communities, organizations, or families. The point is, we see, either in the news or immediately around us, examples of people achieving the highest levels of success. But when we look closer, we can see that nearly all of them have done so by specifically NOT following the traditional paths. As the old joke goes, "Did you know that Bill Gates never got his college degree? Imagine how much richer he'd be if he had?!"

So many people continue to judge their own progress and success by a linear model of success. In our society, we are taught that progression through life, particularly a successful one, is on some sort of linear path with clear markers and directions. That there are progressive developmental phases that you are supposed to go through, starting with birth and ending with death. That one's trajectory is to be positively correlated with becoming older, better educated, more experienced, etc. If you are not following in these tracks, then somehow you are off track, not performing well, a problem in need of solving.

In a linear model, you are failing or somehow off course if you are not in the right place in life at the right time, with the right amount of success that various externalized measures deem you should have. Think of the judgment many of us have of someone over the age of eighteen who doesn't have a high school degree, or people in their late twenties who haven't finished college, or in their thirties

UNLEASHING FROM THE CORPORATE MINDSET AND THE LINEAR ILLUSION OF SUCCESS

but still living with their parents, or in their forties but still don't know what they want to be when they grow up. These are strong social stigmas. Conversely, you can be too far ahead of the game if you are experiencing success before you should be, such as the twelve-year-old college graduate or the twenty-year-old billionaire CEO. We glorify them but then quickly question what the real story must have been. Therein lies the judgment that we constantly endure from outside ourselves, but likely also place upon ourselves as well. we are not successful if we are not mapping according to some predetermined linear trajectory of success.

Even if we account for a few setbacks or the "take one step back to take two steps forward" model, we still end up evaluating against a trajectory that slopes ever upward, like the examples below. The key here is that in the linear model of success, we feel good or bad about ourselves depending on where we perceive ourselves to be on that never-ending upward slope.

Misconceptions of success

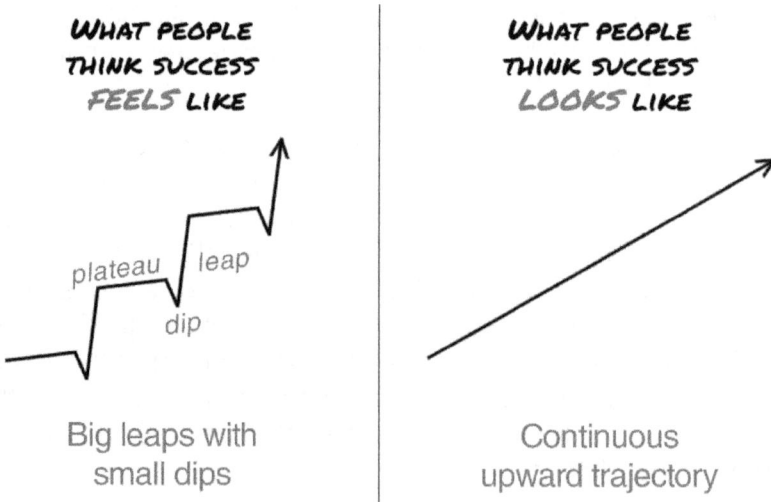

Somewhere deep down, though, we all know that none of this is quite right. Success is not the absence of challenge, conflict, or life lessons. In fact, it is all of those life lessons that shape our unique brand of success.

UNLOCK THE CORPORATE MINDSET

If you do not feel like you are on the right path, then you probably aren't. However, that may not be because of anything that you did or didn't do, but because the proverbial path of success that we put everyone on is simply not designed for everyone to succeed! Feel free to get off at the next stop.

The path of linear success in life is an illusion, if for no other reason than because much of what correlates success with age, developmental phases, and time is accounted for by all of the societal rules about who can do what, at what time in life (e.g., play, compete, vote, work, lead). That is not to say that life cannot follow a semi-linear path for some people or that there is no truth to the progression of developmental phases. But clearly there are many myths and societal expectations that continually feed the illusion of the linear progression of life—and in particular, a "successful" life. These myths warrant consideration and deep reflection before we choose to allow ourselves to be subjected to their measurements, expectations, and judgments. Further, should we choose to use it as a guide for our own personal development and evaluation of self, we should make damn sure we understand it and embrace it fully.

Rejecting The Non-Rules Of The Corporate Mindset

The corporate mindset teaches us many things that, by this point, we have hopefully proven to be incredibly flawed, if not altogether false. However, as part of the process of awakening, some rules are harder to shed than others, especially as we apply them to ourselves. The reality is that all of the rules of the corporate mindset are entangled, no single rule can be true if the others are false, and no single rule can be false if the others are true. So, as we work to shed ourselves of the entire set of rules placed upon us by the corporate mindset, it is often a good exercise to review the falsehoods it puts forth and ensure we are prepared to reject all of these rules, knowing that acceptance of even one as truth may leave the door cracked for others to come creeping back in. So, as a reminder, here are ten rules of thumb that the corporate mindset asks you to believe are true:

Ten non-rules of the corporate mindset

1. Success is linear.

2. You are what you "achieve."

3. You need more experience to be great.

4. Winners bootstrap their success and no one helped them.

5. There is room for only one person at the top.

6. If you play this game long enough, you will win.

7. Titles and pay matter and directly indicate ability level.

8. Be a good team player but achieve individually.

9. Those who hold you accountable are working against you.

10. What goes up must come down.

UNLOCK THE CORPORATE MINDSET

Before we completely reject these rules out of hand, first ask yourself how many of these rules you believe. Why do you believe them? How has believing in these rules supported or aided you, to date?

As we continue to work to reject these rules, pull back the veil of the corporate mindset, and stop showing up at the corporate ball, our own personal truths will begin to shine through and become our new norm. We begin to see the "matrix" for what it is. After enough moments of truth, you may even have the experience of watching others operate inside the grid but feel completely outside of it yourself. It is almost as if the world is moving and rotating around you. Further, you might start experiencing moments where you feel like the universe shifted just for you; something amazingly positive will happen that is in total juxtaposition to the rules of the corporate mindset, and the only reasonable explanation for why, is that things just cannot be as they seem.

If this is starting to sound a little freaky and New Agey, and maybe even a little religious, that's fine. From within the context of the corporate mindset, it certainly is all of those things. These concepts simply cannot be true in a world filled with the rules and standards of success that make up the corporate mindset and the linear illusion of success. But, we can assure you that those very rules to which so many are attached look just as weird and unsettling when they are viewed from the other side.

Shifting To Your Own Model of Success

Living our lives by leading well and achieving our goals for ourselves and for humanity—that is the goal, right? Not to live and die by the achievements at work. Not to fulfill the vision of someone else. It is great to be successful at work, but it is not healthy to make work our singular end goal. Staying focused on our own goals and how we want to impact the world is far more important.

Let your work achievements simply reflect your progress toward your life goals. The real question that we all have to hold ourselves accountable to on our deathbed is, "Did I do it right?" Did we live meaningful lives? Did we accomplish meaningful things? Did we leave positive legacies for our family and others?

Most people choose to accept a linear or semi-linear model of success simply because they lack any other models to use. But it is critical that we not measure ourselves by the models of others. Even if you have knowingly, or unknowingly, bought into someone else's model, then surely the successes and failures of that model belong to someone else and don't really belong to you. What does it matter if you are losing a race that you are not even trying to run? Or, conversely, to win a game that you are not really trying to play? To actually be successful, however we define it, we must first be clear and in accordance with our own unique beliefs, values, and models of success.

We should take a moment to acknowledge that to the extent that a person's beliefs, values, goals, and model of success differ from the normative linear standard, they may be subjected to questioning, judgment, ridicule, and considerable discomfort from others. But, this is the work we must do and why many people are reluctant to make the changes they need to be happy and successful. If we are able to tap into our individual truths and know our own model of success, then it really begs the question of why we would ever use outcomes and metrics of another model with which we probably don't even agree.

Finding one's own model of success can be a challenge. But if we are not going to tout our degrees, wealth, size of homes, and number of cars on our deathbeds, then why lead that way? Consider the questions listed below; they will provide some structure or at least a good starting point. For many, these are not easy questions to answer. But they are the key aspects we must clarify as we consider how to refine our model of success and map the milestones, outcomes, and metrics to our own personal model.

Key questions for developing a personal model of success

- Do you have a personal model of success? If so, what is it? If not, what does success really mean to you?

- On a scale of 1–10 (1 = not at all, 5 = somewhat, and 10 = very much so), to what extent do you feel that you are able to live into your own model of success?

- What are the components that can be measured in your model of success (e.g., number of close friends, income, countries visited, etc.)?

- So that you can live more fully into your own model of success, what is one thing you can do more of? Less of? That you should continue doing?

- On a scale of 1–10 (1 = not at all, 5 = somewhat, and 10 = very much so), to what extent are you comfortable with managing the expectations others may have of you to perform within their definition(s) of success?

There are those who have come to understand that life is not on a linear path and jokingly refer to the messiness of it all. Life IS messy. But, what if it is messy for all the right reasons? What if there is a method to all that messy madness? Rather than a linear approach, perhaps your journey through life could be better understood through a more cyclical model that allows for and leverages the messiness.

Measuring Your Truth, By Your Truth

One final note before we move on, and that is something we see all too often as people embark upon this journey. Even after people have become disenfranchised with the corporate mindset and they set off to embark upon their own path, one of the greatest challenges and barriers that people struggle through is that they continue to judge their success in their new space by the very metrics of the corporate mindset. Egad! That is certain to lead to feelings of failure and insecurity because you are using measures that were never meant for you, and were certainly never meant for your new model. You can't decide to live outside the matrix and continue to measure your personal success by the principles of the matrix. Well, you can. But, it's going to suck!

It is critical to realize that once a person rejects the non-rules of the corporate mindset the model shifts, and so too does the evaluation of one's sense of progress and success. You don't have to have your model completed up front to feel comfortable navigating outside of the corporate mindset, but it is important to note this phenomenon so that you do not get sucked back in.

So, to recap briefly, we have now revealed the corporate mindset and its effects, debunked the linear model of success, and begun our journey to create our own unique model of success. From here on in, the real work starts: finding how to fully live into our own unique brand-new model of success. When you're ready to manifest this change and live on the brighter side of leadership, just take a breath and flip the page.

THE EVOLUTION TO RADICAL LEADERSHIP

> **DON'T BE INTIMIDATED BY WHAT YOU DON'T KNOW. THAT CAN BE YOUR GREATEST STRENGTH AND ENSURE THAT YOU DO THINGS DIFFERENTLY FROM EVERYONE ELSE.**
>
> **—SARA BLAKELY**

In our society, which largely subscribes to a survival-of-the-fittest capitalist system, the expectation is that only a select few will thrive and reach the top. Darwin tells us this within the animal kingdom and genetics, so it seems reasonable to apply it to the human condition. Further, statistics tell us about bell curves and how most of us should simply expect to be lumped somewhere in the middle.

It is an audacious move to challenge Darwinian theory, basic statistics, or the processes of natural selection. So, to be clear, what we are positing here is not a challenge to these scientific truths, but rather the flaw in applying them to the human condition and determinations of success as a one-to-one relationship.

What if you were not designed to be average? What if you should not be herded to the middle? What if the middle in one model could also be the very top or bottom of other models? Consider the possibility that everyone, including you, has exceptional and totally unique talents and strengths. That each of us is designed to balance and leverage each other's strengths like an interlocking puzzle, where each individual piece has a place within the whole for which it is uniquely designed to fit. So, not survival of the fittest, but a fit that is necessary for our collective survival.

What if the only reason we do not see the remarkable talents of others and ourselves is because we condition ourselves to feel that they too are average, or even less than? But if it is our true nature to be exceptional, then we must create the space for everyone else to be their truest selves, as well, so that we can all shine and benefit from each other's strengths. We call this being authentic, and we previously spoke of authentic leadership. But we have learned that

THE EVOLUTION TO RADICAL LEADERSHIP

for those in the corporate mindset, being authentic feels like a radical shift, and so we acknowledge it as so.

In truth, it is not radical at all. In fact, it is only radical when placed in juxtaposition to the corporate mindset. It is, in fact, a model that allows you to simply and continuously be your most awesome and amazing self, each day, and for the rest of your life. The journey is really about making a clear commitment to your definition and model of success and developing the practiced discipline to navigate the journey.

The 11 cycles of evolution to the brighter side of leadership

Cycle 1:   Superpowers Activate!

Cycle 2:   Get The Freak Out Of Here

Cycle 3:   Risking It All, But For All The Right Reasons

Cycle 4:   Who First? Me First?!

Cycle 5:   The Trust Factor

Cycle 6:   Where Is Your Finish Line?

Cycle 7:   The Fear of The Illusion That is Success

Cycle 8:   Turn Fear Of Conflict Into Windows Of Opportunity

Cycle 9:   Being Accountable To You

Cycle 10:   Your Authentic Presence As A Leader

Cycle 11:   Success On The Brighter Side Of Leadership

Now that you are at the crux of unlocking from the corporate mindset, we are going to take a different approach. In turning the corner, there is a rather dynamic process that you must navigate to effectively flip the game on itself. The components to the evolution of the brighter side of leadership are not steps but cycles of evolution.

In each of the following cycles, you will find an introduction and overview of the step; key actions you can take to master that process; an example of how we have worked with everyday

UNLOCK THE CORPORATE MINDSET

leaders, just like you, to progress from one cycle to the next; and a worksheet for you to follow along.** If you find yourself wondering why you are reading examples from everyday leaders and not from top-performing Fortune 500 CEOs, then we ask that you revisit the last two sections. Focusing on people because of their title is simply not how we think. Let's be honest here, you are probably not a top-performing Fortune 500 CEO. And even if you are, the model of success for some other CEO is only a single model. Thank goodness it worked for them, but why limit ourselves to that, when there are so many other real examples of leadership done well, and you can be your own best model?

*Let us not play the game.
Let us beat the game until the game itself disappears.*

Once you have mastered each of the cycles, you will have mastered you! You will no longer be dependent on the corporate mindset. It will become an illusion, and you will be free to lead on the brighter side of leadership, as you were always meant to be.

** If you would like to print out any of the action step worksheets, rather than completing them in the book, they are available at www.tandemspring.com/unlockworksheets

1 SUPERPOWERS ACTIVATE!

Cycle

To bring your whole and authentic self to the table, you must be able to embrace all of you. For some, this might require a little bit of therapy or coaching, but it ultimately requires a shift at the most core of levels. The most effective way to do that is to activate your superpowers and let your strengths outshine all of your deficits and negative thinking. We're going to take a minute to look at what that really would look like and how you can do it yourself.

Activating your strengths

Embracing our true power requires transforming ourselves and our thinking toward a more positive and strengths-based way of understanding ourselves. Most people know what it means to be more positive; "look at the world through rose-colored glasses" or "the glass is half full" perspective. But, being a superhero/ine requires more than that; it requires what we call an "Olympian" mentality. It is the mentality that is strong enough not just to win, but to excel beyond expectation! Truly living life from strengths means shifting how we see ourselves and operate at a level others might only be able to dream of!

And like any transformation, it starts with the mind—and more specifically, the way you see yourself. The first step is to acknowledge the talents you already have, those gifts that you were born with. This seems like it would be the simplest step, but it is often one of the most challenging. Asking people to list their talents and strengths is kind of like asking a group of teenagers if they have any questions: you often get nothing back but blank stares and rolling eyes, even when you were sure you'd get tons of eager hands shooting up to the ceiling.

Ask yourself, right now: What are your talents? No, really—say out loud your top ten talents right now. We'll wait . . .

It's kind of tough, isn't it? Well, we're going to fix that. This next exercise will help you come up with a clear understanding of your strengths and talents. Let's start with talents.

Listing your talents

Sit with a pen and paper and list characteristics and skills that you feel are your unique talents. These can be anything—anything at all. It can be unique or common. It doesn't matter. Just keep listing. Don't discount anything for being too simple, like having a great smile, infectious laugh, being a helper, an organizer, or a nurturer, being high energy or competitive, etc. Include fun talents, like singing, dancing, being athletic or comical. The key is to come up with as many as you can without judging yourself. You can't write down too many. When you think you're done, challenge yourself to write a few more until you have totally exhausted your brain.

As you work through building your list, keep in mind that to get the best possible list, you need to:

1. Actively release the stereotypes and judgments you may have internalized about yourself. If you get stuck doing this, feel free to email us your entire list of negative thoughts at unproductiveBS@tandemspring.com and we will take them and purge them for you.

2. Turn off the negative voice in your head so you don't overlook, minimize, or discredit any of your talents and strengths. You don't want to miss a single one!

3. Now, flip on the positive voice inside of your head and turn the volume to 11!

Need a little help? Try texting some of the people closest to you and ask them for two or three things they think you are best at.

Owning your strengths

The next step is to list your strengths. Strengths are those talents that you have mastered over time. They are usually some combination of your raw talents and areas that you have mastered over your lifetime through training, learning, overcoming challenges, and just living (e.g., relentless problem solver, master organizer). Recognize that it is not uncommon for a strength to be born out of hardship. Like muscles, talents often need resistance to grow and develop into strengths.

THE EVOLUTION TO RADICAL LEADERSHIP

If you're having trouble identifying your strengths, a great way to get some help is through assessments. There are a number of them, but we like the ones listed below. If you have taken similar assessments before, feel free to pull them out and write those characteristics below your talents.

Action Step: Take A Strengths-Based Assessment

- CliftonStrengths (formerly known as Clifton StrengthsFinder)
- VIA Character Strengths
- Authentic Happiness

Actualizing your true power

Now that we have lists of our talents and strengths, the next thing we need to do is figure out how to actualize our power. That is, how do we live into these talents and strengths and make them part of our daily lives?

Actualizing is about becoming your true self and realizing your full potential. This is where you get to put on your personally customized superhero/ine cape, a quilt of your special talents and unique strengths, and become your own superhero/ine. Think about it: there may be a person out there with whom you share some talents and strengths, but NOBODY will share your unique combination of talents and strengths, and that is what makes you so unique and so super! To activate your true power, you will need to delineate the behaviors that best exemplify your combined talents and strengths.

Unapologetically living into your superhero/ine strengths

With your list of talents and strengths, you have the foundational tools you need to make the transformation. But the key now is actually *doing* it. Revisit your strengths over and over, and keep them top of mind and yourself accountable to them every day.

To relentlessly overhaul your mindset to a strengths-driven orientation, the key is persistence. First, develop a plan by taking your lists of talents and strengths and figuring out how you can make them the driving force behind your every thought and action.

What would you need to do differently? What should you start doing, or stop doing? Start by making sure you live into your plan as fully as you can for just one day. Then challenge yourself to do it for a week, then a month, and so on.

Becoming a superhero/ine is WAY more than just seeing the world through rose-colored glasses; it is a manner of living into and truly owning your power in the world. So activate your strengths and engage your power. Soon you will be your own superhero/ine, leveraging your strengths to help the world become a better place, in the way that you have always envisioned.

Superpowers In Action

In working with a leading female who was starting her third career, we had to shift from the deficit-oriented thinking that she picked up in her first two careers and elevate her mindset to a strengths-based perspective so she could more effectively sit in her role as a leader.

The start-up she was running was a great idea, met the needs of the market, and offered a solid product. The key barrier was that the product was slightly ahead of the market by a few years. For the leader, this meant that she had to find a way to sit forward as an industry expert in a way that she never had to do before and, frankly, in a way that she initially found to be rather uncomfortable for her tastes. But, for the business to succeed, potential clients had to believe she was the expert and trust her as a new leading voice in their field.

Now, to be clear, both of her previous careers were positive and she had naturally done a nice job of leveraging her strengths, but she did not give herself full credit for what she had accomplished. In a beautiful way, she just saw herself as doing what was necessary to take care of her family. She would often demure that she just worked hard, got a little lucky, and had good support. But, as one of the leading women in her industry, it was critical to reevaluate her journey through strengths to fully capture her superpowers for what they were.

THE EVOLUTION TO RADICAL LEADERSHIP

She wasn't lucky—she was prepared. Because as we know, luck favors the prepared.

After taking the CliftonStrengths assessment, we realigned her strengths in a way that was more productive for her. She could see much more clearly what she brought to the table that had allowed her to be so successful in the past. Further, by understanding her past through strengths, she could much more readily see how she could tackle her new endeavor through those same strengths. She knew why people should follow her and believed that what she was offering, and the way that she was offering it, was the best model out there. She had her superpower cape. And now, she's happy to go toe to toe with any CEO or leading thinker in her industry. As a result, not surprisingly, her business is steadily building sustainable momentum and she is increasingly recognized as a leading thinker.

Superpowers Activate Action Step

Take a strengths-based assessment.

We have provided 3 excellent options to take a strengths-based assessment below. Complete at least one of the following.

CliftonStrengths
(formerly known as Clifton StrengthsFinder)

- https://www.gallupstrengthscenter.com
- $19.99 or $89

CliftonStrengths is offered by Gallup and takes about thirty minutes to complete. For your efforts, you'll receive your Top 5 Strengths out of a list of thirty-four strengths, along with details on those strengths and insights on how you might be operating through those strengths today. You also gain access to an electronic copy of the StrengthsFinder 2.0 book for further reading and insights into strengths. If you want, you can unlock all thirty-four strengths for a total of $89, but the Top 5 is more than enough for most people and certainly good enough to start with. Originally developed by Donald Clifton, widely acknowledged as the Father of Strengths-Based Psychology.

VIA Character Strengths

- http://www.viacharacter.org
- Free, $20, $40, or $50

The VIA Character Strengths Profile is free, takes about twenty minutes, and you'll get a stack ranking of your twenty-four character strengths. The full report, which details how your strengths benefit you and gives tips on using your strengths, will cost you $20. The VIA PRO Report, which is a more in-depth twenty-eight-page guide to your strengths, including how to manage overuse and underuse of strengths, will set you back $40. They try to upsell you to get both for $50, but don't bother—you just need one or the other. Developed with oversight from Martin Seligman, widely acknowledged as the Father of Positive Psychology.

Authentic Happiness

- https://www.authentichappiness.sas.upenn.edu/testcenter (Select the "Brief Strengths Test")
- Free

The Brief Strengths Test from University of Pennsylvania's Authentic Happiness Program is free, takes about five minutes, and shows how you compare to others across the same twenty-four character strengths provided in the VIA Character Strengths assessment. This gives a more indirect result for your strengths, but is still quite useful if you can't or won't spend the money on one of the assessments above. Does not provide any sort of report, but you can learn to understand your results better by buying Martin Seligman's book, which they try to sell you after you take the assessment (usually for about $10 on Amazon).

List your top 5 strengths here:

_____

_____

_____

_____

_____

GET THE FREAK OUT OF HERE

Earlier, we looked at the deep disenchantment most of us have with our jobs and how we masquerade who we really are and how we really feel in the name of fitting into the corporate culture. In this section, we'll tackle what to do to extract ourselves from such situations. And the answer is incredibly simple and yet complex: act authentically and let your freak flag fly.

Envision a different reality in the workplace. Aim to challenge the corporate mindset to want more, expect more, and do more. To flip the game in the right, healthier, happier, and more authentic direction. We call it **The Corporate Mindset Challenge** [as said in the quintessential booming announcer voice] or CMC for short. CMC exists to challenge businesses to reflect the people who run them, while also challenging the people who run those businesses to authentically operate in their strengths. By doing so, they in turn allow everyone else in the organization to operate in their own unique strengths. So, let's be clear:

1. When we refer to the people who run companies, we are referring to you. Please do not forget that. Businesses are nothing more than a collection of people, and it is the people who make companies successful. People are not their titles or their paychecks. They are their talents, strengths, and lived experiences. The essence of what people have to offer is rarely captured in a title, regardless of whether their title is CEO or graveyard shift part-time junior associate intern.

2. To operate in your unique strengths does not mean that you just continue to pump up the same old things you think others want to see from you. In fact, it's quite the opposite. It's about showing up in that outfit you love but thought was too funky for the workplace, or in your next meeting saying that thing you've been dreaming of saying but could never bring yourself to say. Remember Soul Train? Remember those crazy dance moves and outfits? Do you think those people making their way down the line dances were concerned with what others thought or

THE EVOLUTION TO RADICAL LEADERSHIP

judged them on? No way! Those were people letting their freak flags fly—those were people living into their unique strengths and talents. If you've forgotten, just hop on YouTube and search for "soul train line dance." We'll give you a minute . . .

3. When you let your freak flag fly, you exude a refreshing clarity about who you are and what you have to offer in a way that automatically lifts the veil off of the corporate bullshit and makes it so much easier for you to be you and for others to authentically engage with you. Often this is so true that you'll see tangible improvements in your communications and productivity in a very real way almost immediately. If companies could truly unleash your potential instead of squash, squelch, and squander it, a lot of the challenges that prevent us from excelling and thriving in our work would simply melt away.

4. Leaders of organizations, by title, are people, too. As such, they should be held to the same standards as everyone else, if not higher ones. However, CMC requires that CEOs be held not just to the same standards but to also sit side by side with their employees, as colleagues who simply have identified and lived into their unique strength of being a leader and the face of an organization. Comparatively, the employee is someone who has the strengths of accounting, administering, technology, sales, etc. All strengths, and quirks, are equally valued within the community of people who choose to work at the enlightened organization.

5. To the extent that your particular organization can't handle your freak flag and likely tries to squash it, leave and get the freak outta there.

For many people, there is comfort in owning their strengths, but it is often uncomfortable to fly your freak flag. The challenge is that when a person is not comfortable flying their freak flag, they often build deficits and inefficiencies into their model of success (e.g., "I really want to run the company one day, but I am too scared to tell anybody that that is my real goal. Instead, I'll create an alternative and humbler path to success that doesn't let anybody know what I am really thinking or trying to do."). Why would we not go for what we really want, if what we want is authentic to who we are, grounded in strengths, and tied to how we want to positively impact the world?

Think back to the viral sensation in late 2013 of Marina Shifrin publicly resigning from her job at Next Media Animation via interpretative dance to "Gone" by Kanye West. Don't remember it? Well, sadly, the original has been pulled due to copyright issues with the song, but you can still view the countless videos about the original video all over YouTube. Think that's too bold? Yeah, it might be. But then we also have to ask why the whole world banded around this young woman? Her video, before being pulled off of YouTube, gained nearly twenty million views. Why? She also received a very public job offer from Queen Latifah on her television show. That's never happened to anyone we know. Why would that happen? We think it is because the world knows the suffering she was enduring and loved her for flying her freak flag high and proud.

"What about burning bridges?" we often hear people say in their concerned response. But burning a bridge to a place you'll never go again ain't quite so bad. Not doing so leaves ties to something that very well may be toxic to you, your career, and your soul. Why stay and tolerate that which isn't tolerating you? Is it not clear that, over a long enough timeline, it is simply not going to work out for you there? Don't try to find ways to fit your freak into their box just to maintain a paycheck. And if you do choose to do that, please don't also kid yourself by looking for meaningful engagement and happiness in your work. Go find meaning and happiness first, THEN find a way to get paid for doing what you at least like, if not love. Or, just create your own space and really get your freak on.

THE EVOLUTION TO RADICAL LEADERSHIP

Action Step: Complete The Corporate Mindset Challenge (CMC) Questions

1. On a scale of 1–10, to what extent are you really able to lead through your strengths in your current job(s)?

2. How many times a week do you fly your freak flag at full mast?

3. What would your title be if you could really fly your strengths freak flag? Get creative; don't use corporate titles to define something that may sit WAY outside of the box.

4. On a scale of 1–10, looking at your average day, to what extent do you feel you are living in a way that will result in genuine meaning and value to you?

5. On a scale of 1–10, to what extent do you think your responses to these questions are impacting your engagement with your work?

There are no right or wrong answers to these questions. But your answers should be illuminating and hopefully spur you into action. If you are struggling with what to do next, read on as we jump into activating your superpowers.

Freak Flags In Action

We worked with an individual who had recently started his own consulting business. Deep down, he aspired to have his consultancy be the gold standard in its niche. But he had concerns that as a new consultancy, he wasn't yet ready to be in the spotlight and take on the exposure needed to get to the top of his field. This leader had many years of making a name for himself and was extremely well liked and respected. Major media outlets would reach out to him for his expert opinion on matters, but he would choose to keep his head down and "focus on his business rather than the fame."

After a few months, the media outlets stopped calling, and opted instead to get quotes and articles from his competition. This, of course, drove him mad. He often exclaimed, "Why would they talk to that idiot!" After his dissatisfaction with the "incorrect" perspectives that were being put forward by his competition grew large enough, he had to compose letters to editors and contact outlets about why what they had just published was inaccurate or incomplete. It took two years of solid effort before the reporters would reach out to him as they previously had. But when they did, he held nothing back. He told them exactly what he thought and minced no words. By doing so, not only did he get the model and perspective of his consultancy front and center in the discussion within his industry, he was also now heavily sought after for his candid "no bullshit" approach. From there, it was no surprise that his consultancy grew and is considered by many in his field to be leading practice.

It was only when this leader was finally willing to admit to himself, to the media, and to the world that he really thought he was the single best person in his field that everything started coming together for him and for his business. Until he was willing to fully fly his freak flag, the world just kept turning and simply waited for him to come to the table with his truth.

THE EVOLUTION TO RADICAL LEADERSHIP

Get The Freak Out Of Here Action Step

Complete The Corporate Mindset Challenge (CMC) questions.

1. On a scale of 1–10, to what extent are you really able to lead through your strengths in your current job(s)?

   1   2   3   4   5   6   7   8   9   10

2. How many times a week do you fly your freak flag at full mast?

   _____ times per week

3. What would your title be if you could really fly your strengths freak flag? Get creative; don't use corporate titles to define something that may sit WAY outside of the box.

   _____

4. On a scale of 1–10, looking at your average day, to what extent do you feel that you are living in a way that will result in genuine meaning and value to you?

   1   2   3   4   5   6   7   8   9   10

5. On a scale of 1–10, to what extent do you think your responses to these questions are impacting your engagement with your work?

   1   2   3   4   5   6   7   8   9   10

Printable worksheets are available at www.tandemspring.com/unlockworksheets

3 RISKING IT ALL, BUT FOR ALL THE RIGHT REASONS

The question then remains, why should you bother with all of this? Why not just stay content with the way things are and leave all this hard work to be done by someone else?

There are a variety of answers to this, and for each person it is a little different. But between the voice in your head that tells you the rules you are living with are misguided and the strong downside risk of staying inside a system like that, there are reasons to do the work.

We've discussed at length the voices in our head and how to recognize our truths. We now want to take a moment to talk about risk. Most people view the corporate mindset and operating inside the matrix as the "safe" choice, the less risky option compared to rocking the boat with everything we have proposed here. But we truly believe the greatest risk in life is to stay where we already know we are not happy!

Is it your time to exit the corporate mindset?

How big a risk you are taking by staying in the corporate mindset depends on how bought in you are or are not—how loud that voice in your head is.

Action Step: Answer The Readiness To Leave The Corporate Mindset Questions

1. Do you have to take a deep breath to bolster yourself before actually step into the office?
2. Have you tried several jobs and organizations and none of them seems to work for you?
3. Do you find yourself questioning your sanity at work, wondering if it is "you" or "them"?
4. Do you feel you have an established career but still lack meaning in your life?

5. Are you attracting the people, work, and opportunities you want to see in your life?

6. Do you feel you have lost your sense of self?

7. Do you think your measurements of self-worth are the right ones?

8. Do you find yourself doing things in the name of escaping and/or making your submission to the corporate mindset more tolerable?

9. Given your responses, on a scale of 1–10, how ready are you to leave the corporate mindset?

There is great strength in knowing when to move, and supreme comfort in knowing that the move you make does not have to travel in any direction but your own. So whether you are just starting or well on your way, it is important to continue to reevaluate these kinds of questions to ensure you are continually moving in the right direction, in the direction of your truth. Even as we go through our journeys and begin to live from a new truth, it can still take several more moments of realization and subsequent revelations for your spirit to be open and comfortable in living into its full capacity. The timeline can vary, depending on how far you have to travel into your truth and how many barnacles you have picked up along the way.

The exit door is right in front of you

Well, actually, it is right inside of you. You are your own door and pathway up and out. Over the years, many people have asked us how we were able to overhaul our lives; align our purpose, passion, and strengths; and synergize our business model around joy. And, while we've stepped through a lot of the frameworks and thought patterns, perhaps the two most important things for each of us were (1) putting ourselves first toward a collective end, and (2) being accountable to ourselves, our goals, and our dreams with the understanding that if we did what we do well enough, then we would have everything we needed to help others more fully.

Simple enough? It sounds it, but usually isn't. So, we'll delve a bit deeper into these ideas in the coming cycles.

The Rewards Of The Right Risk In Action

A couple of years ago, I was at an event and was introducing myself to a person I had never met before. They shared that they were unhappy at their job and already knew their passion and strengths, but was fearful of leaving a good-paying salary behind. In response, I shared my story of leaving my job and fiancé, starting a nonprofit, getting into a doctoral program, and launching my career as a consultant, all in just three months. The response was sheer astonishment, immediately followed by them telling me that I clearly must be a "huge risk taker."

It was clear in that moment that despite this person's admiration for my accomplishments, they felt the need to regress back to some preconceived notion of risk, to assuage themselves for not having done anything similar.

In response, I hastily blurted out, "Oh, no! It is YOU who is taking the risk."

I was not trying to be sarcastic or mean. It was just a natural response as I truly believe that the greatest risk we can take in life is to stay where we already know that we are not happy. Certainly, little will come from submitting to a struggle that is guaranteed to have no reward.

I'm pretty sure that at this point this poor person really didn't know what to do with me. But we ended up having a fantastic discussion about what risk is and isn't, and how redefining the word "risk" might help them and countless others to reevaluate their current conditions.

THE EVOLUTION TO RADICAL LEADERSHIP

Risk It All, But For All The Right Reasons Action Step

Answer The Readiness To Leave The Corporate Mindset Questions.

1. Do you have to take a deep breath to bolster yourself before you actually step into the office?

    Yes   No

2. Have you tried several jobs and organizations and none of them seem to work for you?

    Yes   No

3. Do you find yourself questioning your sanity at work, wondering if it is "you" or "them"?

    Yes   No

4. Do you feel you have an established career but still lack meaning in your life?

    Yes   No

5. Are you attracting the people, work, and opportunities you want to see in your life?

    Yes   No

UNLOCK THE CORPORATE MINDSET

6. Do you feel you have lost your sense of self?

   Yes   No

7. Do you think your measurements of self-worth are the right ones?

   Yes   No

8. Do you find yourself doing things in the name of escaping and/or making your submission to the corporate mindset more tolerable?

   Yes   No

9. Given your responses, on a scale of 1–10, how ready are you to leave the corporate mindset?

   1   2   3   4   5   6   7   8   9   10

Printable worksheets are available at www.tandemspring.com/unlockworksheets

4 Who First? Me First?!

The greatest barrier to people sustaining the journey of unlocking the corporate mindset is that someone convinces them or has already socialized them into thinking that by putting themselves first, they are being selfish and/or detrimental to the functioning of the team or family. Well, selfishness, cockiness, and narcissism can certainly be detrimental, but putting yourself first for all of the right reasons will only help you to be a more productive leader.

In truth, it has been our experience that always putting others first is the single best way to ensure that you will NEVER have what you need to really be of value to others. You run out of steam, shortly followed thereafter by running out of sanity. All of this compromises your capacity to really be supportive to the people that you wanted to help in the first place. As self-care expert Eleanor Brownn, puts it, "Rest and self-care are so important. When you take time to replenish your spirit, it allows you to serve others from the overflow. You cannot serve from an empty vessel."

Action Step: Flip Your Model Of Giving

Flip your model of giving toward a Me First model to allow more space for you to have:

- What you need physically, mentally, and spiritually
- A clear vision that conjures the kind of engagement you want to have with others and the world around you
- A power circle of support for your personal vision and goals
- Reciprocal relationships with clear understanding of the benefits for all parties, regardless of one's role
- Boundaries of what real support and help look like, so that it does not breed dependency but instead fosters and continuously inspires growth and development in all parties

Showing up and showing out

Putting ourselves first allowed us to show up and show out in our lives in a way that propelled both of us into new spaces with greater opportunity, and with more authentic connections, simply because we stopped masquerading and were living life out loud. We demanded of ourselves, and of each other, to be excruciatingly clear on what we were looking for so others couldn't be confused about what we wanted and where we were headed.

When you show up and out for yourself, you attract those around you who are living with similar courage, while often intimidating those who aren't. With the right types of people around you, and the wrong types of people choosing to not be around you, you can now work to truly build a dynamic system of support with others who are authentically leading in their own lives. You'll be able to give and take in an honest and mutually beneficial way to and from one another. The boundaries will be easier to identify, navigate, and sustain. You will find endless amounts of energy to be you and with far less effort.

And here are the real benefits to putting yourself first and showing up and showing out:

- You will inspire others to do the same
- They too will generate their own positive energy and power circles, which is likely to not only expand their resources, but also begin to give back to you in meaningful and powerful ways
- One way or another, your load will be lightened
- More importantly, your impact will expand, as will your resources
- Your joy center will have more energy in its power pack…and, in time, you might actually generate some energy reserves!

The key is to realize that it all starts with you! You first, and them second. But in the end, the result is you and them living more fully, together!

Actively Putting Yourself First In Action

A senior nonprofit leader came to us running dangerously low on fuel to continue in her role. Her energy was all but gone, but she still couldn't convince herself to get off of the hamster wheel of putting everyone else first. She was buying into the corporate mindset rule that we must always help others first, regardless of our own condition. It was her reality, and now she was finding herself in survival mode.

We had to ask this leader, this amazing person filled with great potential and strengths, to hand over her giant sack of to-dos and burdens. Literally, we wrote down each and every one of them, to the point of exhaustion. It was a very long list. And then, figuratively, we all agreed to let this bag-o-responsibilities sit on our automated backup system. She could come and pick them up whenever she wanted to. But, for now, she didn't have to concern herself with all of this. "So, now what?" we asked.

For the first time in years, we called her own goals to the forefront of her life. Based on her strengths, we resynergized her natural talents and skills with her passions and dreams to create a model for impact. We then created a list of criteria to help her evaluate and prioritize all of the to-dos, requests, and responsibilities in a way that kept her progressing on her goals through strengths while simultaneously achieving the goals of her organization.

This leader became so much more productive at work and at life that it created more space and time for her to truly be there for family, friends, and community. She was able to revisit some of those old to-dos but now was selective about which ones she wished to take on. She became someone who lives in her spirit and now can lead and support others from her overflow.

When you put yourself first, for all of the right reasons, you ensure that you will be in the best possible position to be of service to others and that you will have the energy to sustain that model of leadership, because it is your model of leadership with your own needs at the forefront.

Who First? Me First?! Action Step

In the spaces provided below, consider what you need to do more of, continue doing, and/or do less of to flip your model of giving toward a Me First model to allow more space for you to have:

- What you need physically, mentally, and spiritually
- A clear vision that conjures the kind of engagement you want to have with others and the world around you
- A power circle of support for your personal vision and goals
- Reciprocal relationships with clear understanding of the benefits for all parties, regardless of one's role
- Boundaries of what real support and help look like, so that it does not breed dependency but instead fosters and continuously inspires growth and development in all parties

Do more of:

_____

_____

Continue to do:

_____

_____

Do less of:

_____

_____

Printable worksheets are available at www.tandemspring.com/unlockworksheets

THE TRUST FACTOR

The next most difficult step to keeping ourselves on the journey of unlocking the corporate mindset is surrounding ourselves with the right people. People often pay lip service to the importance of keeping the right people around but then surround themselves with people who drain their energy and distract them from their greater purpose. We must take some responsibility for having a circle of support if it is not productive in its current form. Now, this doesn't mean that you have to get rid of everyone in your life who isn't clearly serving you and your goals. But, you do have to get clear on who is who, and you might want to evaluate their positions in your life, if only to understand whether you can "trust" them to support you, your goals, your journey, and your impact.

The big question is, can you have a productive relationship with this person in your life? One that is supportive to you becoming a better leader? We could call this owning your power circle or building your tribe. But, we have found that the key factor driving any productive support system is trust. Further, for us personally, a big part of trust was finding a way to evaluate trust and proactively protect ourselves, our energy, and our journey of unlocking from those who might not come through for us or perhaps even work to derail our progress.

Mistrust is one of the top crushers of any new idea, business, or dream. Be it across family, founders, board members, investors, and countless other people involved in those early and most fragile stages of an organization, much of the discord really just boils down to a basic lack of understanding. While good, healthy conflicts should surface during moments of development and growth, if they lead to a break in trust, the effects can often be dire.

Trust can be tricky. We usually learn to redraw our trust boundaries only after our trust has been violated. In other words, we often don't give much thought to trust—whether we should trust someone more or less—and just let the chips fall where they may. Then, after someone does something that compromises our trust in that person, only then do we react and reduce or reevaluate our trust. Most of us tend to be fairly trusting, until we aren't. Which, in and of itself, is a beautiful thing. But a single experience of violated trust can bring us to question the values and standards that we use to guide our interactions and lead us to question any, or even all, of our relationships.

What we propose is that we find a way to evaluate trust in an ongoing way, to avoid these violations as much as possible, and provide ourselves with greater security and comfort so that we can continue our journeys with less fear and misunderstanding. Of course, establishing criteria for trust must be done through the lens of strengths.

Evaluation of trust and trust factors

The challenge and opportunity is to proactively look at the **trust factor** as a critical component of all of our relationships and to do so up front. We do not do this with an aim to be critical. Rather, we are seeking to be responsible to both ourselves and to the other party in how we engage.

In our work, we use a ten-factor trust evaluation model. The factors range from how "ride or die" a person seems to be to how much fun we have when we are around them. For each factor, we take rough estimations on a 1–10 scale, add them up, and then see how the scores shake out, depending on whether we are looking to partner, collaborate, or bring the person on as a client. We try our best to acknowledge what we don't know and then work to learn more and dig deeper into those areas. Too low of a score, and we just might walk. But, it is important to point out that we would do so for all of the right reasons.

It sounds harsh to some, and such a finite model may not be for everyone. But, two things are important to note here: (1) you likely do this at some level already in your head (you're not friends with everyone for a reason—if you instantly distrusted someone when you first met them, ask yourself why and how you do this), and (2) put simply, it just works. Moreover, one of our beliefs is that most people need to spend more time taking long, hard looks at the people they live and work with to ensure they are surrounded with positivity and support. We all know people who surround themselves with precisely the wrong type of people, who make them miserable. Who wants to live like that?! Why not surround yourself with precisely the right kind of people, the ones who make you happy and strong?

So, while we're happy to share the factors we use (see pages 85 and 86), we encourage you to spend time thinking of what the key elements are for you that make up a good friend or coworker. Feel free to take from our model, but the likelihood that your factors are exactly the same as ours is extremely low. Once you get clear on your initial set of factors, test them on a few people you know well and see if the scores make sense. If not, ask yourself what is missing and add those factors to your model. Our model began with just six factors, but it quickly grew to ten and has stayed at ten for a few years now.

Action Step: Develop Your Initial Set Of Trust Factors

1. Compose a list of at least five factors that inspire trust in you.

2. Test those factors on three people you know well.

3. Reassess your factors and add or remove factors as needed.

In our world of developing early and growth stage businesses and business leaders, this exercise is of even greater importance. Finding the right cofounder or early employee can literally make or break a company. And while the key attribute that brought you to a person (be it a specific talent, connections, money, etc.) can be a huge asset to a small business, the less desirable qualities can absolutely doom an enterprise. So we encourage our clients to use this all the time, even to assess us as service providers to them. If we're not a match, let's find out now!

In all, we share this here simply to bring awareness to the idea of putting structure to our relationships and engagements, allowing us to be more accountable to our own needs and the needs of our businesses. We believe such honest reflection could benefit a lot of people, even those who might end up on the short end of such an analysis—it's a learning, and they can grow from it. Honesty hurts only when you're not ready to hear it.

If, in the end, being so quantitative with others is not for you, that's fine—no judgment. But if you are serious about your journey of awakening, ensuring that the people around you are the right type of people can often be the most supportive and freeing step you can take in the process. Remember, you are trying to break from a pervasive and entrenched mindset, change yourself, find your truth, and put yourself first. If you are constantly being slowed by those around you, you very well may never get to where you are trying to go. Instead, find a way—any way—to surround yourself with people, things, and energy that will consistently motivate you in the direction you are trying to move.

> ## Trust In Action
>
> A female business leader who had come to us felt like she had to manage two sides of herself. One was the positive, fierce, and charismatic start-up leader, while the other was the much more passive person she felt she had to be around her family. The challenge was that it was splitting her personality in two and becoming too much to manage every day.
>
> More specifically, she felt she had to maintain this less intense side of her personality for people who were not particularly trustworthy. These individuals were often intimidated by, and therefore unsupportive of, the more positive, engaging, and charismatic side of her personality. She didn't know how to integrate her leader side with her family side, as her family had only known this one side of her personality for so many years. It felt unsafe to bring her whole self to the table, and this was causing her to second-guess which version of herself was even the real her anymore. What type of leader was she, really?
>
> Leveraging strengths and the key components of her personality that were working well, we created space for her to integrate her sense of leadership and realign her power circle. We created trust factors and rated the key people in her life against her new model of evaluating trust. It was clear: those closest to her, the ones she engaged with the most each day, were simply not supposed to be in her power circle. They just

THE EVOLUTION TO RADICAL LEADERSHIP

didn't get it. They didn't get her. While upsetting, it was okay to acknowledge this, realign expectations, and engage with these people differently moving forward. Once she put the changes into place, everyone benefitted, not just her—her whole family appreciated the realignment of expectations and the changes in her eventually allowed for space to be created for the right people to show up in her life!

She is now much more whole, is the leader she wants to be, and has deep trust in her network to help her to elevate as a leader, in life and in business, while still maintaining positive and productive relations with her family. But it all began with evaluating trust and making the necessary shifts.

The Trust Factor Action Step

Develop Your Initial Set Of Trust Factors.

1. Compose a list of at least five factors that inspire trust in you. (we've given you room here for up to ten)

    1. _____   6. _____

    2. _____   7. _____

    3. _____   8. _____

    4. _____   9. _____

    5. _____   10. _____

2. Test those factors on three people you know well.

    In the table below, put the initials of three people you already know well in the left-most column. Then, evaluate that person on a 1–10 scale for each factor you identified in Step 1. Total their scores in the right-most column.

	Factor 1	Factor 2	Factor 3	Factor 4	Factor 5	TOTAL
Person 1						
Person 2						
Person 3						

Printable worksheets are available at www.tandemspring.com/unlockworksheets

3. Reassess your factors and add or remove factors as needed.

    Consider the results from Step 2. Do they look right? Is the person you think is most trustworthy the person with the highest score? Does anything need to be added or removed? Keep repeating this process until you feel really good about your factors and how they shake out with the people you know today.

Printable worksheets are available at www.tandemspring.com/unlockworksheets

TandemSpring's ten-factor evaluation model

As referenced above, here are our ten factors for evaluating potential partners, collaborators, and clients. We use this so often, we just say the name of the factor and we all know what it means. But as these will be new to you, we've provided the key questions that we ask ourselves when considering each factor's score.

- **Strategic**: Can you see the bigger picture or do you lose the forest for the trees? What are the biggest problems you can solve while still seeing all the angles? Would anyone consider you a strategic person? Are you any good at chess?

- **Ride Or Die**: Can you be counted on, no matter what, to show up and contribute? Are you really committed to the team? When you're tired and just don't want to do one more thing, do you have the ability to suck it up and do it anyway?

- **Confidence**: Do you know that you know your shit? When you walk in a room, does everyone notice? Do people listen to what you say, not even necessarily because what you say is good/smart, but just because of how you say it?

- **Down For The Journey**: When times get tough, are you going to double down and bust through or shrivel up like a bitch? When you take off, will you still be around or will you leave us in your dust? Are you mentally and psychologically prepared for all the ups and downs of entrepreneurialism?

- **Expertise**: Are you an expert? Is the thing you do something that you have proven you are great at? Do you bring a unique skill, talent, knowledge, or industry depth that is a value add to the team?

- **Fun**: Do we want to be around you? Are you just fun to be around? Do you bring an energy to the group that we want and enjoy?

- **Spirit Of Excellence**: Is the shit you produce top-notch? Do other people in your space talk about how incredible you are? Are you always seeking to deliver above and beyond anyone's expectations?

THE EVOLUTION TO RADICAL LEADERSHIP

- **Values**: Do you believe what we believe? Do we share values? Do the values you have resonate with us? Do we aspire to be more like each other, or is how you look at life all kinds of crazy to us?

- **Leadership**: Can you lead? Will people listen to you and can you take on the responsibility of being a leader? Are you aware of your leadership strengths, and are you currently able to live into them? Can you communicate effectively from a position of leadership?

- **Network Activation**: Do you know people and have a network? Moreover, can you make that network DO? Who do you know and what can you really make happen with those people?

WHERE IS YOUR FINISH LINE?

We've discussed accountability to self and keeping the right people around us, but to make those as effective as possible, we have to get clear on what success means to us at a very personal, individualized level.

As previously highlighted in our discussion of the linear illusion of success, many people are operating from an externally defined model of success that does not fit their lives or their goals and wonder why they do not feel successful. It was suggested that one must measure success in accordance with one's own life, beliefs, and values. Crafting your milestones and key metrics based on your own unique path and model of success eliminates the illusion and makes your goals and objectives much more tangible and meaningful for you. That is what we are going to try and achieve in this cycle.

Action Step: Unpack And Name The Linear Illusion Of Success

1. List your top five personal and professional goals.

2. Name each goal in terms of where it came from (e.g., mine, work, family, parents).

3. Prioritize the goals in accordance with your Me First model. If needed, revisit your answers from the Who First? Me First?! Action Step in Cycle 4.

4. Evaluate those goals that are not yours and do not fit within your Me First model and remove as necessary.

5. Redefine any goals that you would like to keep but are not yet serving your broader vision for having a positive impact on the world around you.

6. For each goal that remains, assign an ideal percentage of time that you would like to spend working on it.

THE EVOLUTION TO RADICAL LEADERSHIP

Below are a set of principles that many of our clients find helpful to keep an open mind to the many other possible ways individuals can define success for themselves. Feel free to use some, all, or none of these as you consider your own model of success.

Guiding principles to defining your own model of success

1. **True success can be defined only from within oneself.** You are the only one who truly knows your talents and strengths and how you want to use them to get what you want out of life. Therefore, you are the best expert in the world on what accomplishments will have meaning to you as you navigate your success.

2. **The trajectory of success is never linear.** One's success is determined by a whole slew of factors (e.g., talents, strengths, training, opportunities, resources, luck) that evolve over time. The evolution of those key factors in our lives is almost never a linear path. At a minimum, it has its ups and downs. But, most often, it is a cyclical path that tends to feel like one is moving forward, reflecting, and circling back around to only move forward again. For some, this may feel a little all over the place, and it may be, but that hardly makes it bad or wrong.

3. **Success is not necessarily an upward trajectory.** True success is not becoming the biggest and baddest at something unless that is truly who you are designed to be and what you are truly designed to do. For most of us, that is just not the case, however appealing it may sound up front. Instead, most of us will experience the greatest happiness and joy by focusing on becoming who we are designed to be and achieving an optimal level of engagement in the world around us. It is tracking toward a more complete sense of self, and not a comparison of self relative to some externally defined model of success. This is more of a horizontal, never-ending line with the current self on the left and the whole self on the right. You want to continually move to the right in pursuit of what is likely a moving target and an unattainable perfection. But with each move you are improving and progressing, albeit not necessarily "upward" or toward being the greatest at anything other than being the greatest at being you.

4. **The process of becoming one's self naturally leads to a transcendence beyond self and into the collective.** Remember Maslow's Hierarchy of Needs from earlier? Well, the top level is called transcendence for a reason. If you follow your own model of success in a full and complete way, your success becomes contextualized beyond yourself and grows into the collective community. This is what transcendence and real impact are all about.

5. **The process of becoming one's self is never complete and is a forever-evolving journey.** As long as one is living authentically in the process of awakening, becoming one's optimal self is never done. There is no gold star at the end of the journey that indicates that one's growth toward becoming a whole and complete person within our society is complete. There is always more work to do. But that is actually the most beautiful part in all of this; there is no final level of achievement, so there is always something to work on, to hone, and to improve.

So where is your finish line? We can't tell you. We know where ours are, but nobody can tell you where your finish line is. The great thing is that not only is the answer within you right in this very moment, but the answer will provide you with the meaning, happiness, and joy you have been seeking!

Finding Your Finish Line In Action

A client came to us trying to figure out how to get his business on track. He was a young man, fresh out of college, with a very successful start-up. He had won awards and plaudits and was committed to building a multimillion-dollar business. He worked tirelessly to grow the business and achieve success. After a few sessions, he said he wanted to now go and raise a few million dollars in venture capital, as that would validate that his business was really worth something. So he began to pursue that with his special degree of vigor. A couple of weeks later, he wanted to close a massive deal that he had on the table.

THE EVOLUTION TO RADICAL LEADERSHIP

This trend continued for a few months, and after a number of these gear shifts, we finally took a breath and asked, "Success seems to keep being right around the corner for you, but never quite here as you try to accomplish this or attain that. What is it that you are REALLY trying to do here?" This was an incredibly difficult topic for him. He was so entrenched in his thinking around building a business, making money, and succeeding that the question of "Why?" was still rather foreign to him. After some deep dialogue and honest reflection, he came to realize that his needs were rather simple: he just wanted his girlfriend—and to a lesser degree, his parents—to love and respect him. He was working this hard, and trying to achieve every milestone, only to gain their love and respect. So, the natural questions were: (1) Does he have their love and respect? and (2) Does building this business help gain their love and respect? So, he was tasked with talking to them and finding out the answer to these questions.

Not surprisingly, the response was overwhelming: not only did they deeply love and respect him, but they were all so incredibly proud of his work. What came up, though, were a few comments about how much they missed him because he was gone all the time working on his business. He immediately realized that his finish line wasn't about building a huge business or making piles of money—it was much simpler than that, and he already had it! A few months later, he had sold a portion of his holdings in his company, changed roles so that he could spend more time with family, and unquestionably reached his finish line.

Sometimes the answers are simple and right in front of us. But, due to deficit orientations, corporate mindset thinking, and simply not taking enough time to see the forest for the trees, we can often miss it.

Where Is Your Finish Line? Action Step

Unpack And Name The Linear Illusion Of Success.

1. List your top five personal or professional goals.
2. Name each goal in terms of where it came from (e.g., mine, work, family, parents).
3. Prioritize the goals in accordance with your Me First model. If needed, revisit your answers from the Who First? Me First?! Action Step in Cycle 4.
4. Evaluate those goals that are not yours and do not fit within your Me First model and remove as necessary.
5. Redefine any goals that you would like to keep but are not yet serving your broader vision for having a positive impact on the world around you.
6. For each goal that remains, assign an ideal percentage of time that you would like to spend working on it.

Use the table on the following page to complete the above steps. Feel free to cross things out, erase, or redo—there are no bonus points for getting it exactly right on your first try.

THE EVOLUTION TO RADICAL LEADERSHIP

	Where It Came From	Priority With Me First Model	Ideal Percentage Of Time
Goal 1			
Goal 2			
Goal 3			
Goal 4			
Goal 5			

Printable worksheets are available at www.tandemspring.com/unlockworksheets

THE FEAR OF THE ILLUSION THAT IS SUCCESS

As we work to define our finish line, it is imperative that we not be sidetracked by our own false perceptions of success. We've done nice work to this point to leave the corporate mindset and the linear illusion of success behind. But that doesn't mean we can't still be tempted by false aspirations, often leftover remnants from previously subscribing to the corporate mindset. But when we dig into these aspirations, at the heart of them we usually find negative emotions—most typically, fear.

As we've discussed, we live in a world ruled by the false perception that the linear illusion of success is a real thing. The result of this is that most people are terrified of "failing" because to do so means we are somehow behind others or we'll never achieve success. Where things get particularly crazy is when we add on to this fear of failure a second fear: the fear of success. Most people have heard of the fear of success but don't know exactly what it means. In short, it means holding on to fears associated with being "too" great for friends, family, community, and loved ones.

FEAR IS NOT THE OPPOSITE OF SUCCESS—
IT'S A PART OF IT.

—WILLIAM RITTER

It is easy to say that we'd like to switch places with Mark Zuckerberg or Bill Gates or whatever other billionaire-type you can think of. But would you, really? Honestly, how would that actually feel? What would your friends and family think of you? Would you still be you? Are you really as comfortable with that kind of exposure, fame, envy, and notoriety as you think you are? Further, consider the concepts we use in our society like being called a "sellout" or "getting too big for your britches"—where do these ideas even come from? They are the calling cards of the fear of success, and when we buy into them and combine them with a fear of failure, we limit ourselves to a very narrow band in which we can be comfortable operating. When you consider the vast range of existences one can have in a lifetime, it can be startling to realize how many of those realities would be deeply unsettling to us because they have too much or too little power, money, fame, etc. This is the combined effects of the fear of failure and the fear of success at play. It is a very maddening world that we have created where people can't be happy if they fail or succeed, and yet we are still expected to wake up each day and do amazing things!

The never-ending cycle of fear

As a society, we have put ourselves into a catch-22. Starting from kindergarten, or even earlier, we are told to "pass" and not "fail" so we can advance. We do this through high school, college, graduate degrees, into the workforce, up the corporate ladder, and then, when we reach some point on this linear path, we are often told that we've gone too far, and we fly into the hands of the fear of success. Many of us spent the first half of our lives trying to make certain that we were more than enough to live up to our parents', partners', and friends' expectations, but then have to switch gears entirely and concern ourselves with being "too much." Doesn't this all just sound terrible?! What the hell is going on?

Underlying expectations

When asked about the fear of success, most people talk about the expectations that their parents had of them when they were young and their concerns about meeting those expectations as adults. Some have internalized expectations of other family members or friends. If we are really looking for transformation in our lives, then it is time to liberate ourselves from the expectations that we think others have of us.

First, expectations built off of an illusory model of success can't be real, because that game isn't even real. Second, those who love us just want us to be happy and to make the best decisions for ourselves. It is such a truthful cliché that we often forget it and instead revert to teenage rebellion against even the most modest of well-intentioned suggestions. That said, when we are free to fully reflect, we find that much of the time it is not that others have come to us with expectations, it is ourselves. Even in cases where parents did have strong expectations of us as children, they often have grown and shifted; as a result, so, too, have their expectations of us. It is we who continue to carry that burden, regardless of where our parents or other loved ones now stand.

There are three types of people in our lives with expectations:

1. **False Expectors:** These are individuals who have their own unresolved issues, and their expectations of you are really about them—what they wish they would have done, their insecurities in not living life the way they really want to live, etc. The harmful effects of these people are not to be underappreciated or oversimplified; they can be quite toxic and can truly make for a difficult journey. Even if you are able to live up to their expectations, it is very unlikely to make them happy and instead may make them more jealous, frustrated, and angry.

2. **Supportive Expectors:** There are supportive people in your life who also have expectations of you. But their expectations are genuinely derived from a loving place of wanting the best for you. That being said, their understanding of what is best for you probably derives from their own life experiences and as a result may not always be applicable to your journey. Their expectations may also be informed by what they heard you say, and any gap between your expectations and theirs may be more about miscommunication than a pressure to perform. Some people might also correctly hear and understand your expectations, and the accountability they are asking from you is truly for your benefit. Supportive expectors can be turned into accountability partners through open dialogue, communication, and clarity about your goals and ways that they can best support you. However, it is important to note that the responsibility to have the conversation is yours, as these are your dreams and goals we are talking about. Nobody knows them better than you. But enlist the help of a coach if you need assistance in getting them out of your head so you can articulate them clearly for others.

3. **You:** More than anyone outside of ourselves, it is usually our own mental formations that have led us to set expectations, whether inspired by internal or external influences. We are not to blame for the circumstances that imposed, infused, or imprinted these expectations, but we are responsible for seeing the grid behind the matrix of these expectations. Finding our own way out of the insanity is our responsibility, not because we have to pull ourselves up by the bootstraps or any of that nonsense, but because the true sense of empowerment must come from within. When expectations come from inside of you, they build into a perpetual opportunity for you to become the person that you truly want to be.

Action Step: Identifying Your Expectations And Your Expectors

1. List five people close to you in your life.
2. Identify at least one expectation each person has of you.
3. Label the expectation as false or supportive.
4. Determine whether each person is a false or supportive expector.
5. List any expectations that truly come from inside of you.

Evaluate those goals

The most important truth in all of this is that often the power needed to transform expectations of you is quite simply already in you. Albeit difficult, bear in mind that the performance expectations other people have of you are not real, are often falsely imposed or irrelevant to whom you really want to be, and can be in direct juxtaposition to your own values and vision for your life. To find happiness, sanity, and real measures of success, we must find a way to move beyond our self-imposed limitations about our own capabilities to perform. The answer is to become empowered from within by turning meaningful expectations into personal goals, all while leveraging your strengths to achieve those goals and move forward with great clarity, force, and intention.

Redefining Expectation In Action

The story of a long-standing friend and client clearly illuminates the positive and negative sides of expectations. When we first met, he was launching a start-up, finishing graduate school, and recently married. The expectations were immense: he was to be a good husband, first and foremost, but then also succeed in a very difficult graduate program, all while building what could become an incredibly lucrative and highly technical business. Needless to say, this was a lot. In fact, it was too much. He had expectations of himself, to be sure, but he also had a wife and business partner who, as it turned out, were actually strong false expectors in his life. This perfect storm of expectations simply became too much for anyone to bear.

Through an admittedly very painful but remarkably short process of just a few months, he left school, his business, and his wife, and thereby freed himself from a number of false expectations that he was taking on, including his self-inflicted ones. Once freed, he was led to a profound journey of rediscovering his truest intentions.

His journey began with getting clearer on what he wanted to do with his life. Not long thereafter, he had found a girlfriend who was considerably more supportive in her expectations of him and often plays the role of accountability partner to him today. He then leveraged our trust model to further clarify his network of support and found he had some great resources right under his nose that he wasn't fully appreciating. This then led to him to launch a new business, one far more closely tied to his passions and beliefs. On all fronts, he is now doing wonderfully. He is joyful and successful but in ways that could have never revealed themselves without him first freeing himself from a myriad of negative expectations.

In short, by clearing out a number of false expectations, including ones he was placing on himself, reorienting around his most honest expectations, and surrounding himself with supportive expectors, he is now on a considerably more authentic and joyful path in life.

The Fear Of The Illusion That Is Success Action Step

Identifying Your Expectations and Your Expectors.

1. List five people close to you in your life.
2. Identify at least one expectation each person has of you.
3. Label the expectation as false or supportive.
4. Determine whether each person is a false or supportive expector.
5. List any expectations that truly come from inside of you.

Use the table on the following page to complete the above steps. Feel free to cross things out, erase, or redo—there are no bonus points for getting it exactly right on your first try.

UNLOCK THE CORPORATE MINDSET

	Expectation(s)	Is Expectation False Or Supportive?	Is Person False Or Supportive Expector?
Person 1			
Person 2			
Person 3			
Person 4			
Person 5			
You			

Printable worksheets are available at www.tandemspring.com/unlockworksheets

Turn Fear Of Conflict Into Windows Of Opportunity

One of the hardest parts of dealing with expectations, especially those from outside of ourselves, is dealing with the conflict that arises when we choose to no longer abide by those expectations that do not serve us. Here again, fear can rear its ugly head. Fear impacts our ability to progress in our journey by manifesting in the form of conflict avoidance. Rather than address an issue and the potential conflict that may erupt, we choose instead to try to ignore it and live our lives as if it didn't exist. Put simply, this doesn't work. But it especially doesn't work when we are trying to live into our truest selves.

One of the biggest productivity crushers for individuals and for organizations is conflict avoidance. Conversations are never had. Challenges go unaddressed. Projects are delayed. Time, money, energy, and often even relationships are all forever lost.

Is there a choice in conflict?

It is important to realize that having a conversation, however difficult, is not conflict. It is the avoidance of conversation that creates conflict.

Challenging conversations do not have to stop us in our tracks, so long as we can come to see them as opportunities for growth and development. A challenge becomes a conflict only when people are unwilling to have the conversation and instead opt to let things go unresolved in the name of avoiding conflict and keeping the peace. It is the decision to not talk and to let things go unresolved that ultimately results in a fiercer conflict in the end.

Everyone has challenging conversations and while they may be unpleasant in the moment, most of us can look back on these hard conversations and realize that, for the most part, we grew, learned, or found a deeper connection with someone. Even those conversations that ended poorly and may have even changed the course of our lives, such as breaking up with a significant other, usually have led us down a path that we are later grateful for.

If you go through a day without a conversation that has challenged you in some way, you are either lucky or unlucky, depending on how you choose to look at it. Many people perceive challenge as negative. In truth, challenges are positive or negative, depending on how they are perceived, applied, addressed, and resolved. The same is true for a challenging conversation. The fact that a conversation is difficult does not make it a conflict, even if emotions get involved. Countless difficult conversations have led to new insights, lifelong lessons, and unforeseen opportunities. Once the discussion has been had and the lessons have been learned, most conflicts can be a net positive for all parties involved.

Waving the red flag

Conflict is also not an indicator that something bad or wrong is happening. If we are truly on the same team, then navigating difficult conversations is not only normal but an expected part of the journey. We're not the same person. We don't see the world through the same eyes. Most of the time, conflict is just the expression of differences—and that's great!

Further, as we all strive to have comprehensive views and a variety of inputs into our lives, our thinking, and our businesses, we should be seeking real diversity, To achieve real diversity, expression of differing views and conflict of thought are not only expected, but imperative. If conflict is not happening, it means either nobody is talking and willing to have the challenging conversations (which is a major red flag) or everyone on the team thinks alike (an even more major red flag).

Forming, storming, norming, performing

Perhaps the best known and most widely accepted model of group development and dynamics is known as Forming, Storming, Norming, Performing. Originally proposed by psychologist and professor Bruce Tuckman, the theory maintains that each of the four phases are not only necessary but are inevitable in order for teams to grow, face up to challenges, tackle those challenges, find solutions, plan the work, and successfully deliver results. For each and every one of these steps to occur with a diverse set of thinkers, challenging conversations will need to be had. Therefore, what we often refer to as conflict may, in fact, be a signal that our group is growing and maturing just as it should.

Moving from the mind to the body, consider how our muscles are developed. A good trainer will push clients to a point of muscle fatigue to take advantage of the fact that as muscles mend they fortify themselves. Team dynamics are exactly the same. The resolution that comes from navigating tough conversations only makes the team stronger and more cohesive. That being said, the key here is *if we are on the same team*. When we are not on the same team, even simple miscommunications will seem like a conflict worth fighting about (giant red flag number three).

None of this is to say that conflict is fun with a capital F or easy to deal with. But it can bring about positive moments of insight and growth. It requires thoughtful and intentional conversation while listening with your "third ear" or "*ting*," a Chinese word that refers to listening with all of your senses. We must listen in this way to others, as well as to ourselves, so we can effectively explain our intentions and be open to those from others. But even when we are navigating conflict with the greatest of skill, there are many traps in the maze of conflict that you should aim to avoid.

Traps in the maze

- **Avoiding the conversation in the name of needing more time is just an excuse.** Many people need time to think things through and cannot resolve conflict as readily as others. This, of course, is fine and another example of diverse thinking, which is good. Where it turns sour is when people ask for more time than they really need in the hopes the issue will fizzle out and they can escape from the conversation altogether.

- **Having a conversation with yourself (or anyone but the person/people involved) is not having a conversation.** Some people choose to have their own conversation, either in their head or with uninvolved parties, about conflict. They use this to then come to their own conclusions and make determinations about what they are or are not going to do, without ever engaging or informing the party they are having the conflict with. This is a very dangerous practice, as doing so is certain to only reinforce our existing views, even for the most objective of people, and never resolves the real issue at hand or gives the party we have issue with an opportunity to do anything about it.

- **Withholding information from the conversation will only minimize the opportunity for growth and development.** Many people walk away from conversations without putting it all out on the table. This all but ensures that those concerns left off the table will rear their ugly little heads at some point in the future. Further, if the first point of conflict was only partially addressed, then the second point of conflict is likely to seem that much bigger, if only because it now feels like the first problem just won't go away and might be unresolvable.

- **Conflict does not have to be drama.** Many people have a performance that they act out when they experience conflict. These are patterned behaviors often picked up in childhood from watching parents or loved ones have conflict. These performances can add unnecessary fuel to the fire by adding too much drama to the situation (e.g., playing the victim when there is no evidence of victim blaming, shouting, huffing and puffing) or remove heat from a conversation that should have some (e.g., leaving in protest when things really haven't even gotten that contentious). It is not always obvious just how much drama is to be inserted into a challenging conversation, and it must be determined on a case-by-case basis. But we often can sense that a conversation has way too much or too little emotion to it, and we should reflect honestly upon our roles in that.

The key indicator of a conflict gone awry is not the conflict itself, or even the emotions that surface through the conflict, but when the conversation cannot and is not being had. When a conversation cannot be had, then we are certain to stay right where we are. We will not win. We will not see and hear each other. We will not learn about each other, create new processes to help others with a similar problem, or grow. This is how challenging conversations become conflicts and is the most glaring trap of all to avoid.

Action Step: Turn Recent Conflicts Into Opportunities

For at least the last three conflicts you can think of that you had with anyone, be it at home or work, do the following:

1. Give each conflict a name and identify who it was with.
2. On a scale of 1–10, rate how difficult the conversation was for you to have.
3. Identify whether or not the disagreement was resolved.
4. Identify how you primarily engaged in the disagreement. Did you accommodate, compete, compromise, or collaborate with the other side? (see page 110 for definitions)
5. On a scale of 1–10, rate how much value you got out of the conversation.
6. List anything that, upon reflection, you now realize you could have done differently to get more value from the disagreement.

I NEVER LOSE. I EITHER WIN OR LEARN.

—NELSON MANDELA (AND ALSO TUPAC)

From walls to windows in the face of conflict

If you are struggling with having a conversation, ask yourself whether are you worried about the conversation itself or the potential resolution of it—or are you just afraid to initiate the conversation in the first place? Each of these requires different tactics to overcome, but once you become clear on why you are avoiding a challenging conversation, you can usually bring it into the conversation itself. For example:

- If you are concerned about having a conversation because you don't want to hurt someone, you can simply insert language such as, "I've been worried about having this conversation with you because I know it'll hurt your feelings, but . . ."

- If you're worried about the resolution, you could simply say, "I'd like to talk about something, but I don't know if you'll like the resolution I'm going to propose . . ."
- Or, if you are worried about initiating the conversation, just get the ball rolling with something like, "I was worried about bringing this up with you because you often get really upset when I talk about X, but it is important to me that we talk about . . ."

The opportunity in it all

Once you initiate the conversation, most people will engage in it, however good or bad it may feel to do so. If they show one of the traps discussed above, note it and try to work around it but don't let it derail what you need to get done for yourself. Once the conversation is had, the conflict nearly always fades, and hopefully you will be able to get back to doing what you do. But, ideally, you'll be better informed and resolved so you can do it even better than before. If you are part of a team, then your team should function better for having had the conversation. If it isn't, perhaps another conversation, however challenging, is in order. It is only through those difficult conversations that we can avoid real conflict, develop as people and as a team, and really find our paths to success.

Embracing Productive Conflict In Action

An organizational client came to us looking for strategic direction, but it didn't take long to realize that conflict, and the avoidance of conflict, was the real reason for the strategic stagnation of the company. This organization's CEO is a very strong personality, and he knows exactly what he wants and how he wants it. Even minutiae, like the wording of a press release or webpage, had to go through multiple iterations across his desk before it was permitted to go out. But interestingly, there was hardly ever any conflict at the organization, so the leader believed that morale was strong and everyone had, more or less, bought into his vision, management style, and strategic direction.

THE EVOLUTION TO RADICAL LEADERSHIP

As it turns out, this couldn't have been further from the truth. Sessions with team members revealed that they were miserable, felt unheard and underappreciated, and, in many cases, were confused as to what the organization was even trying to do. As coaches and consultants, we were not in a position to set the direction, but knew it had to be brought up for conversation and this would have to lead to productive conflict to find resolution.

Through a number of structured workshops and one-on-one sessions, we strengthened the will of the team members. They began to speak up in meetings, expressing their views, and even their disagreements with the CEO. To be sure, this was not immediately well received by the CEO, who didn't understand why everyone was "against" him all of a sudden. But through patient conversations, it became clear that they were all on the same team and these disagreements came from a place of love for the organization, its mission, and for one another as coworkers.

After a couple of months, the office had a completely different feel to it. It was lighter and freer. Team members were happier and felt more authentically engaged in their work. Perhaps even more importantly, the organization is now doing better than it ever had before, as the diversity of thought led to more productive, innovative, and sustainable operating models. Conflict and disagreement, while perhaps not particularly enjoyable in the moment, led to considerable gains and opened the door to a more satisfying experience for all parties—and even positively affected the bottom line. Can't argue with that!

UNLOCK THE CORPORATE MINDSET

Turn Fear Of Conflict Into Windows Of Opportunity Action Step

Turn Recent Conflicts Into Opportunities.

For at least the last three conflicts you can think of that you had with anyone, be it at home or work, do the following:

1. Give each conflict a name and identify who it was with.
2. On a scale of 1–10, rate how difficult the conversation was for you to have.
3. Identify whether or not the disagreement was resolved.
4. Identify how you primarily engaged in the disagreement. Did you accommodate, compete, compromise, or collaborate with the other side? (see page 110 for definitions of these conflict engagement modes)
5. On a scale of 1–10, rate how much value you got out of the conversation.
6. List anything that, upon reflection, you now realize you could have done differently to get more value from the disagreement.

Use the form on the following pages to complete the above steps. Feel free to cross things out, erase, or redo—there are no bonus points for getting it exactly right on your first try.

THE EVOLUTION TO RADICAL LEADERSHIP

Conflict #1

Name: _____   With: _____

Difficulty: 1   2   3   4   5   6   7   8   9   10

Resolved: Yes   No

How: Accommodate   Compete

                     Compromise   Collaborate

Value Derived: 1   2   3   4   5   6   7   8   9   10

Lessons Learned / How to Improve Next Time:

_____

_____

Conflict #2

Name: _____   With: _____

Difficulty: 1   2   3   4   5   6   7   8   9   10

Resolved: Yes   No

How: Accommodate   Compete

                     Compromise   Collaborate

Value Derived: 1   2   3   4   5   6   7   8   9   10

Lessons Learned / How to Improve Next Time:

_____

_____

Printable worksheets are available at www.tandemspring.com/unlockworksheets

UNLOCK THE CORPORATE MINDSET

Conflict #3

Name: _____   With: _____

Difficulty: 1   2   3   4   5   6   7   8   9   10

Resolved: Yes   No

How: Accommodate   Compete

                  Compromise   Collaborate

Value Derived: 1   2   3   4   5   6   7   8   9   10

Lessons Learned / How to Improve Next Time:

_____

_____

Conflict #4

Name: _____   With: _____

Difficulty: 1   2   3   4   5   6   7   8   9   10

Resolved: Yes   No

How: Accommodate   Compete

                  Compromise   Collaborate

Value Derived: 1   2   3   4   5   6   7   8   9   10

Lessons Learned / How to Improve Next Time:

_____

_____

Printable worksheets are available at www.tandemspring.com/unlockworksheets

Definitions of Conflict Engagement Modes:

- **Accommodate** is when we neglect our own concerns to satisfy the other person. This may be done under the guise of charity or obedience. The other party gets their way.

- **Compete** is when we try to win our position, defend a position we believe is correct, or simply try to be one who is right. We (try to) get our way.

- **Compromise** is when we find some expedient, mutually acceptable solution that partially satisfies all parties, such as splitting the difference or finding middle ground. Neither party gets their way, but both sides have some of their concerns met.

- **Collaborate** is when we work with others to find a solution that fully satisfies, or even exceeds, everyone's concerns, such as exploring a disagreement to learn from each other's insights or trying to find a creative solution to an interpersonal problem. Both parties get their way and have all their concerns met.

Conflict resolution types and their definitions are based on the work of Kenneth W. Thomas and Ralph H. Kilmann, the creators of the Thomas-Kilmann Conflict Mode Instrument (TKI), which is available from and the property of Kilmann Diagnostics.

Being Accountable To You

Clear on expectations, our next step is to develop accountability to those expectations. If we just take a quick step back to reflect, we'll see that all of us have already put in our 10,000 hours toward mastering our strengths. We all have overcome countless fears and doubts in our journey. We have discovered our expectations of ourselves and where they came from, and have chosen to either accept or reject the expectations of others. We've explored how the concept of the linear path to success is an illusion. So why, then, would we not all be operating in our most authentic truth and as our fullest selves? The answer, quite simply is that, at some level, we are choosing to not be accountable to ourselves.

Awww, shit

Think of an unpleasant task that you choose to do anyway. For me, the immediate example that comes to mind is picking up after my dogs, who just love to poop all over our backyard. Now, certainly if I choose to approach this task from a deficits orientation, I can name twenty reasons why this task sucks: it smells, it's gross, it hurts my back to bend over, it's cold outside, and sometimes it gets on me (that's the worst!). But, I still do it and, for the most part, nobody even has to ask me to. Why? The answer comes from looking at even such a mundane (and gross) task from a strengths-based orientation. First, I like to get shit done (pun intended). Second, having a nice and clean home and yard is a supportive expectation I have of myself. Last, my top strengths are Command and Relator. In my backyard, it would be pretty tough to relate to people, much less command them, if it stinks from mounds of dog feces. So I pick up after my dogs.

It's a trivial example, to be sure, but the point is important. When we think of accountability, we usually mean it in the context of doing something we don't really want to do but feel like we *have* to do, usually because someone else is forcing us. This, clearly, has negative connotations all over it. And as a result, accountability often feels pretty terrible.

THE EVOLUTION TO RADICAL LEADERSHIP

No more sour lemons

If we can couple accountability with our strengths, the whole lens through which we see accountability flips. We now enjoy doing the task at hand because it is tied to the things we find important, expect from ourselves, and are best at—even if the task itself isn't directly correlated to the strengths in question (e.g., I'm not particularly talented at picking up dog shit—I would hardly say it is one of my great strengths). Imagine if the task at hand was not only tied to what you consider to be important, but also to your strengths. What you now call "work" may just transform into a meaningful task, get done more quickly, and even have a more successful outcome. Dare we say it—you might even start to have fun!

Once we begin to look at accountability in this way, it becomes much easier to be accountable to ourselves. Moreover, once accountable to ourselves, we can put ourselves first and thereby have enough strength, time, and energy to be of value to those around us. So, as we discussed earlier, if you really want to be of help to others, put yourself first, and for all the right reasons.

Action Step: Transform Work Into Meaningful Tasks

1. List five tasks you completed in the last day or two—these can be anything, however important or trivial.

2. Indicate on a 1–10 scale how much you enjoyed doing the task.

3. Identify at least one strengths you used or could have used in completing the task.

4. Consider how you might use more of that strength in completing that task next time.

5. Identify how you could bring in other strengths next time you complete the task.

6. If you were to do what you say in Steps 4 and 5, then on a scale of 1–10, how much might you enjoy doing the task next time?

Secret sauce

The secret sauce in accountability is accountability to self. While we spend countless hours of our lives pleasing others, accountability toward others is really only the second part of the equation. If done passively (i.e., just performing tasks for others) and not actively (i.e., leveraging your strengths to accomplish something meaningful to all parties), then it results in a pseudo-empowerment that allows us to receive praise from others and feel good for having done something—anything. However, if that something did not hold value for us, then we are still left feeling empty, as if we had not done anything in the first place. Or worse yet, that we just expended all that energy for no reason.

Five things to create space for your real empowerment

- Stop making your perception of other people's expectations your excuse to not be accountable to yourself.

- Stop saving others while drowning in your own pool of madness.

- Don't put your job responsibilities before your own personal sense of empowerment. And if/when you do, please don't expect it to generate any real meaning or momentum in your life.

- Stop making excuses for why you didn't show up for yourself (e.g., worrying, deflecting, squabbling, criticizing or blaming self and/or others).

- Find and understand your daily barriers to achieving your optimal level of performance or upper limit (e.g., feeling fundamentally flawed, disloyalty and abandonment, believing you will be a burden), and work to address them every day.

Perhaps the most important and most positive attribute of being accountable to ourselves is that when we do, we get the things we need. This, in turn, gives us the ability to give others what they need. Only by taking care of ourselves can do our best work in taking care of others. Put another way, every time we choose to satisfy others' needs before our own, we are, in the end, choosing to actually NOT help others as much as we otherwise could.

Accountability To Self In Action

A client came to us complaining about how hard fundraising for start-up capital for her business was. She was an extremely talented CEO with a very compelling business, but it needed money to get off the ground and she absolutely hated having to go around "hat in hand" and "beg" for money. She felt fundraising involved a lot of ass kissing and swallowing of her pride, and she was acutely aware of the sexism being demonstrated to her that her male peers did not have to endure. In all, she was stuck: she needed the money to continue her business, but could not bring herself to do the work of fundraising. She came to us hoping we could "just make the next few weeks happen without my noticing."

By now, you know this isn't exactly what we do.

Instead, we acknowledged everything she said about fundraising, because she was right. Fundraising for a start-up can be demeaning, and doing so as a woman is often rife with sexism. Even leaders of the most successful start-ups find raising capital to be an absolute chore. In short, she wasn't wrong to feel the way she did.

UNLOCK THE CORPORATE MINDSET

Once she felt heard, we started to identify her strengths and how they could be leveraged to "trick" her into doing the fundraising. Turns out, her top strength was Achiever, according to the CliftonStrengths assessment. Achievers just like to get shit done; it almost doesn't matter what it is—they live to cross things off their to-do list. This was easily leveraged. We had her make a to-do list of every single person she needed to make an initial call with—roughly one hundred people. After those initial calls, she was to create a follow-up call list, and so on. With her initial list in hand, it was simply a matter of telling her that she MUST get all of those calls done before the end of the week. Her achiever wouldn't let her not do it. Seventy-two hours later, she had called every name on the list and actually even enjoyed the process.

Finding how to use your strengths to get done what you need to get done is a great way to trick yourself into being accountable and doing even the things you dislike most. We are happy to report her fundraising was successful and she continues to grow the business admirably.

Being Accountable To You Action Step

Transform Work Into Meaningful Tasks

1. List five tasks you completed in the last day or two—these can be anything, however important or trivial.
2. Indicate on a 1–10 scale how much you enjoyed doing the task.
3. Identify at least one strength you used or could have used in completing the task.
4. Consider how you might use more of that strength in completing that task next time.
5. Identify how you could bring in other strengths next time you complete the task.
6. If you were to do what you say in Steps 4 and 5, then on a scale of 1–10, how much might you enjoy doing the task next time?

Use the table on the following page to complete the above steps. Feel free to cross things out, erase, or redo—there are no bonus points for getting it exactly right on your first try.

UNLOCK THE CORPORATE MINDSET

	I enjoyed doing this task (1–10)	Strength(s) I used when I did this task	I could use those Strength(s) more by	Other Strengths I could bring in next time	Next time, I'll enjoy doing this task (1–10)
Task 1					
Task 2					
Task 3					
Task 4					
Task 5					

Printable worksheets are available at www.tandemspring.com/unlockworksheets

Your Authentic Presence As A Leader

With the cycles of development in progress, we now look to become leaders. Again, EVERYONE is a leader. It is not dictated by title or income. It is through being the most authentic version of ourselves, so others can follow in the wake of our unique combination of strengths. This last section of our book is simply shared with you so that you can know what to look for as you step into your role as a leader. These are the signs that you are doing it right and making your way to what we call the brighter side of leadership.

At a recent seminar we were fortunate enough to attend, Billy Jean King emphasized that top athletes must bring their whole selves to the game if they want to win. "Harp on your strengths! Bring all of yourself. Head, heart, and guts," she told the audience. We couldn't agree more.

Authentic presence of leaders

Leaders are responsible for creating authentic positive moments in which people can bring their whole selves to the table. When leadership is working well, the boundary between the personal and professional becomes blurred as people no longer have to wear their corporate masks and are free to engage through the fullness of their values and strengths. They don't sit back to think things over; they take the time to move things forward with great intention. They don't wait for the lunch hour or their cigarette break to have fun or be their true selves. Instead, they are inspired to continue their work through lunch and may even find themselves struggling to "turn it off."

In a positively charged culture, we as leaders can let our authentic presence (AP) shine more brightly. Our AP is shaped by the unique application of our strengths in navigating our life journey. It is an unhindered and unapologetic presentation of our unique strengths. Once we are able to demonstrate our AP to others, they will be able to see when, where, and how to best leverage us and our leadership skills. The beauty of authentic presence, in contradiction to executive presence (EP), is that it is not dependent on age, years of work experience, professional accomplishments, or any of that. It is holistic and comprised of all our personal and professional experiences as a leader, as a person who has strengths to offer the world. It is the presence that we carry when our "head, heart, and guts" are synchronized.

Action Step: Get Clear On Your Authentic Presence

1. List your top five strengths.
2. For each strength, consider how your strength is seen by others.
3. How could each strength be best leveraged by those you work with?
4. What kind of people will appreciate this strength?
5. What kind of people might not appreciate this strength?
6. What is your indicator that you are authentically presenting this strength to others?

Responsibility of leadership

When it comes to our AP, we also carry the responsibility as a leader to ensure we bring our best selves to work, rather than worrying about how we'll perform in front of our peers or others. This ensures we will be in the best position to offer our unique strengths to others, unfiltered and authentic. Similarly, others will be in the optimal position to receive our strengths. Work becomes dynamic and engaging, because everyone is in their best place to offer their own strengths and talents to the goal(s) at hand. Further, because they are operating in their strengths, each person will have the AP necessary to individually drive toward a successful outcome, alone or as part of a team, all from the model we helped to set. The opportunity to drive impact becomes maximized, and strengths will be used to drive innovation and overcome barriers as the old tendencies of chasing deficits cease to be considered a reasonable option. This is the experiential goal of the future innovative workplace.

Lead well

Being an authentic leader creates the opportunity for others to stop masquerading at the corporate ball. Where you have one, you will have others. This kind of leadership inspires people to follow and then to lead in their own right. The brighter side of leadership is inherently infectious. Robert Johnson of The Solomon Group coined the phrase "Lead well." We consider the brighter side of leadership the ultimate culmination of people and organizations, together, leading well.

> ### Authentic Presence In Action
>
> A young man was running a technology business and was having trouble with his cofounders. He is deeply empathic and highly relational. He knew this coming in, but we affirmed it with the CliftonStrengths assessment where his results were Harmony, Adaptability, Empathy, Arranger, and Includer. As we dug deeper into his team's issues, it appeared to boil down to two things: (1) he felt the dynamic between him and his cofounders had shifted in a negative way, and (2) this shift had led to a breakdown in trust.
>
> As we explored this further, we discovered that as the business blossomed, he and his cofounders all felt compelled to focus more on the work that needed to be done, and spent less time just hanging out, connecting, and getting to know one another more deeply. Not surprisingly, for this individual who is so heavily oriented around relationships, this was a difficult transition. But, his cofounders, who were much more strategic thinking and executing types, seemed to have lost sight of the value of connecting in this way.
>
> Our client was tasked to have some real conversation with his cofounders, collectively and individually, to see how they felt about this shift. To his pleasant surprise, most expressed a desire for more connection and considered doing so an important element of building and maintaining trust. One cofounder, however, had actually enjoyed the shift away from

so much relating and felt like they were finally doing "real work" instead of just "sitting around chatting all day." Despite this singular dissent, the team agreed to do more socializing and even bought a kegerator for Friday afternoon happy hours, which they began at 3:00 p.m. so everyone could still leave by 5:00 p.m. for their own personal plans. The lone dissenter rarely came to the happy hours and within a few months left the business for another start-up that was a better fit for him.

The point of this story is not about who was right or wrong, or an endorsement or condemnation of happy hours. Instead, it is about the fact that all the leaders in the organization had an opportunity to express what they needed individually for a healthier work environment. For all but one, it led to a positive and productive opportunity to connect, against which they built a plan and executed. For the remaining cofounder, it presented a moment of authenticity against which he could make his own strengths-based decision and ultimately led to an opportunity to find a culture that was more fitting and supportive. One cofounder bringing his authentic presence created an opportunity for everyone to find more space for connection and socialization in ways that worked best for them—for all the right reasons, with truth, and without all the hurt feelings.

THE EVOLUTION TO RADICAL LEADERSHIP

Your Authentic Presence As A Leader Action Step

Get Clear On Your Authentic Presence.

1. List you top five strengths.
2. For each strength, consider how your strength is seen by others.
3. How could each strength be best leveraged by those you work with?
4. What kind of people will appreciate this strength?
5. What kind of people might not appreciate this strength?
6. What is your indicator that you are authentically presenting this strength to others?

Use the table on the following page to complete the above steps. Feel free to cross things out, erase, or redo—there are no bonus points for getting it exactly right on your first try.

UNLOCK THE CORPORATE MINDSET

	How it is seen by others	How it is best leveraged	Who appreciates	Who doesn't appreciate	Indicator of authentic presentation
Strength 1					
Strength 2					
Strength 3					
Strength 4					
Strength 5					

Printable worksheets are available at www.tandemspring.com/unlockworksheets

 # Success On The Brighter Side Of Leadership

We are often asked what we believe success in leadership looks like. Our response has always been the same: it looks a lot like smiling, laughing, and maybe even a little dancing. Of course, there are objective factors of success that we can use to determine if we just had a productive meeting, crossed a milestone, or reached a goal. However, there are also the experiential indicators that we all know are necessary to sustain momentum and achieve meaningful impact that leaders can also monitor as key indicators of success. As an example, here are a few experiential indicators we regularly look for:

- smiling
- laughing
- high fives
- safe space for sharing real emotions
- "a-ha" moments that lead to a getting comfortable with the uncomfortable
- collective moments of truth and transformation
- potential conflict navigated through conversation and dialogue
- open sharing of resources and opportunity
- innovative ideas and creative energy that carry beyond the moment
- celebratory dancing
- sense of community

Action Step: Create Your Own Leadership Metrics Of Success:

1. Identify any current metrics of success by which you are measured in your work.

2. On a scale of 1–10, indicate how important that metric is to you.

3. Add your new metrics of success. Feel free to take from the list above.

4. On a scale of 1–10, indicate how important each of your new metrics is to you.

5. List all the metrics in order of importance.

6. Identify one thing you can do to ensure you meet or exceed each metric.

Certainly, any leader is responsible for performing against metrics, be it growth, profit, cost savings, deadlines, etc. And without question, these are important, especially for those who continue to operate within the corporate mindset. But the great leaders, the ones who lead authentically, also know that without indicators like those listed above in the workplace, getting to those business metrics will, at best, be a short-lived victory.

The Brighter Side Of Leadership In Action Reflection

We worked with a large organization that had one department that really struggled. Performance issues went back years to previous leaders and staff who were involved all sorts of traumatic events, including allegations of racism—the list went on and on. We worked with this team to identify their strengths individually and collectively and then used what we found to broker conversations, some of which were very challenging, to start dealing with the historical issues of the team.

This worked and definitely moved the group forward, but not enough. They continued to struggle with how they should work in this new paradigm and how to identify who was doing good work, being supportive of others and the group, etc. To address this, we did a consensus building workshop for the group that identified the current metrics of success as dictated by the organization and then created a second list of how, from a strengths-based perspective, they wanted to measure themselves. Not surprisingly, the two lists had little overlap.

Two things came of this: First, the group lead was tasked with negotiating some of these differences with the higher-ups in the organization, acknowledging that some of these historical measures were at the root of this group's difficulties. Second, the group created a new set of metrics for their annual reviews.

Now, alongside traditional business measures like quotas and so forth, new measures, including how authentically people are presenting in their strengths and how supportive they are being of others' strengths, are all included in each team member's review, including the group lead. It is measured regularly and can even affect compensation. Moreover, as those metrics are met they are increased, incrementally challenging each person at the organization to work and live more fully in their own strengths and in support of the strengths of the organization. By doing good for themselves individually and for one another, they advance their own growth and that of the business.

If that isn't a brighter side of leadership, we don't know what is!

Success On The Brighter Side Of Leadership Action Step

Create Your Own Leadership Metrics Of Success.

1. Identify any current metrics of success by which you are measured in your work.
2. On a scale of 1–10, indicate how important that metric is to you.
3. Add your new metrics of success. Feel free to take from the list above.
4. On a scale of 1–10, indicate how important each of your new metrics is to you.
5. List all the metrics in order of importance.
6. Identify one thing you can do to ensure you meet or exceed each metric.

Use the tables on the following pages to complete the above steps. Feel free to cross things out, erase, or redo—there are no bonus points for getting it exactly right on your first try.

THE EVOLUTION TO RADICAL LEADERSHIP

Current Metrics Of Success	Importance (1–10)
Metric 1	
Metric 2	
Metric 3	
Metric 4	
Metric 5	

Printable worksheets are available at www.tandemspring.com/unlockworksheets

UNLOCK THE CORPORATE MINDSET

My New Metrics Of Success	Importance (1–10)
Metric 1	
Metric 2	
Metric 3	
Metric 4	
Metric 5	

Printable worksheets are available at www.tandemspring.com/unlockworksheets

My New Complete & Prioritized List Of Metrics Of Success	How I Can Ensure I Meet Or Exceed
Metric 1	
Metric 2	
Metric 3	
Metric 4	
Metric 5	

Printable worksheets are available at www.tandemspring.com/unlockworksheets

Conclusion

So that's it, right? Well, like most things in life, it is never quite that simple. Remember our graphic from the Let's Get Started section of this book? If not, we have it again for you on the next page.

Those cycles in the middle, which we called cycles of learning and relearning life lessons—well, that's what we just stepped through. And what isn't readily shown on a two-dimensional chart is that those cycles are, at least on some level, ongoing and never-ending. That, of course, doesn't mean you'll never get to where you are going or never succeed. Rather, it means that you'll always be aspiring to be even more you. And as who you are changes and evolves, you'll be working to keep up and ensure you are always living into your fullest self. This is a process of uncovering and elevating that has no final resting place. But like any great expedition, it is about the journey and not the destination.

Use each of these cycles as a joyful mechanism to better understand yourself and the world around you. Bring peace and mindfulness to each practice, and, in time (but usually, rather quickly) you'll find that these cycles come and go easily and your progress becomes increasingly effortless. There's a reason the cycles in the graph are depicted similarly to a breath, in and out: because, like breath, you can focus intently on it to improve your breathing and your mind, or you can ignore it, and it'll likely still happen anyways, but perhaps not as smoothly and as healthily.

While we haven't fully reached our destinations, we now have all the tools and resources we need to complete our journeys. Each of us will find the journey to be different, with differing points of challenge and joy. But the outcomes will always be the same: unlocking from the corporate mindset and becoming more fully the person you were always meant to be.

And so, dear friend, this is where we leave you, so you can continue to embark on this journey on your own path. We encourage you to revisit these cycles regularly as a form of accountability to yourself. If you ever struggle or feel off course, please reach out to us. We wrote this book to share our own

THE EVOLUTION TO RADICAL LEADERSHIP

thoughts and journeys, but fundamentally to be of value to others. So, if we can be of further value to you, we sincerely hope you'll let us know.

We thank you for joining us this far into the journey and wish you the very best as you continue down the path of unlocking from the corporate mindset and stepping into the brighter side of leadership.

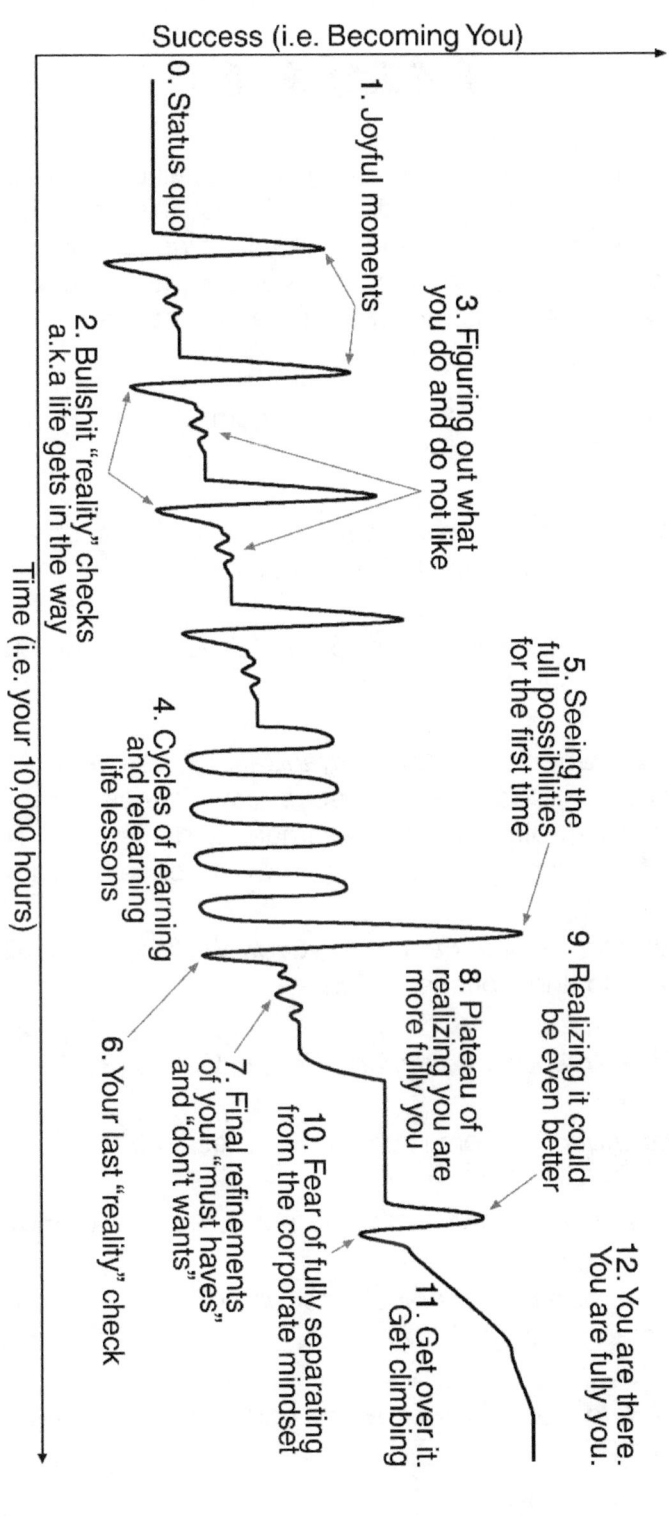

Resources

There are no new ideas. We recognize that all of our thoughts are just combinations and permutations of those that came before. So, we would like to recognize and thank all the wonderful thinkers and contributors who have influenced us and without whose collective wisdom this book would never have been possible.

A Theory of Human Motivation, Abraham Maslow, Psychological Review (1943)

Character Strengths and Virtues, Christopher Peterson and Martin Seligman, Oxford University Press (2004)

Developmental Sequence in Small Groups, Bruce Tuckman, Psychological Bulletin (1965)

DNA of Engagement: How Organizations Create and Sustain Highly Engaging Cultures, Rebecca Ray, Patrick Hyland, David Dye, Joseph Kaplan Adam Pressman, and the 2014 Research Fellows of The Engagement Institute, Conference Board (2014)

Empowerment for High Performing Organizations, Phil Guillory and Linda Galindo, Innovations (1995)

State of the American Workplace Report, Gallup (2017)

StrengthsFinder 2.0, Tom Rath, Gallup Press (2007)

The Art of Loving, Erich Fromm, Harper & Brothers (1956)

Thomas-Kilmann Conflict Mode Instrument, Kenneth Thomas and Ralph Kilmann, Xicom (1997)

Why You Hate Work, Tony Schwartz and Christine Porath, The New York Times (2014)

Download Our Free eBook

Seventeen Terms Redefined From The Corporate Mindset

Inspirational Quotes To Get You Moving

Tips To Get You On The Brighter Side Of Leadership

www.tandemspring.com

About TandemSpring

The best leaders aren't afraid to be themselves—aren't afraid to inspire others beyond their own limitations. If you're ready to realize your strengths and abilities and become a more effective leader, you're in the right place.

Tandem
(tæn·dəm)

Two people that work together to achieve a result.

Spring
(sprɪŋ)

To move quickly and suddenly to a new condition; to cause something to happen rapidly.

TandemSpring
(tæn·dəm·sprɪŋ)

How you get to your next level.